Five Roads to the Cross
according to the Gospels

Five Roads to the Cross

according to the Gospels

ETIENNE CHARPENTIER
AND
MARC JOULIN

SCM PRESS LTD

Translated by Margaret Lydamore from the French
Cinq Chemins de Croix selon les Évangiles
published by Les Editions du Cerf, Paris 1982

© Les Editions du Cerf 198

Translation © Margaret Lydamore 1983

Jerusalem Bible © 1966, 1967 by
Darton, Longman & Todd Ltd and
Doubleday & Company Inc.

All rights reserved. No part of this publication
may be reproduced, stored in a retrieval system,
or transmitted, in any form or by any means,
electronic, mechanical, photocopying, recording
or otherwise, without the prior permission of the
publisher, SCM Press Ltd.

Biblical passages are reprinted from the Jerusalem Bible
by arrangement with Darton, Longman & Todd

The illustrations in the text and on the cover are by
Philippe Joudiou

ISBN: 978-0-334-00486-8

First published in English 1983
by SCM Press Ltd
26–30 Tottenham Road London N1

Typeset by Gloucester Typesetting Services
and printed in Great Britain by
Richard Clay (The Chaucer Press) Ltd
Bungay, Suffolk

Contents

Preface	vii
Introduction	1
The Road to the Cross according to St Matthew	5
The Road to the Cross according to St Mark	25
The Road to the Cross according to St Luke	45
The Road to the Cross according to St John	65
A Traditional Road to the Cross using St John	87
Index of Stations and Passages	105

Preface

Etienne Charpentier died in 2 November 1981, after spending three weeks in a coma following a car accident. His friend Alain Marchadour wrote: 'Those who had the chance of being with Etienne Charpentier were struck by the richness of his personality. Some would speak of his extraordinary capacity for work, and of his gift for putting over the most complex matters very simply. Others would tell of his vitality and enthusiasm, which would erupt at times as from a hitherto dormant volcano. Beyond these more obvious traits, they would all remember his sense of service, his deep humility and his kindness.'

It was in a spirit of service and kindness that, more than a year ago, he undertook to write these 'Roads to the Cross according to the Gospels'. He intended them to be of help to both clergy and laity in finding resources in God's word for the many liturgical celebrations, particularly during Lent and Holy Week. He explains this himself in the introduction he wrote, and which follows this Preface. But he did not complete his work. We had discussed his idea and how it was to be carried out many times, and I have done my best to finish it, keeping as far as possible to his own plan and intentions.

Two of the following chapters, the Roads to the Cross according to St Matthew and St Mark, are written entirely by Etienne Charpentier. He had completed all the commentaries for the Road according to St Luke, except for the introduction, and had left a draft of the prayer guides for the first three sections. For the Road According to St John he had only marked out the stages, and had not written anything. I have therefore completed the Road according to St Luke, and composed that according to St John entirely myself.

However, the series of stations which Etienne Charpentier chose, following an older work by Fr Roguet, are very different from those usually used in parishes, so I thought it might be helpful to include a fifth Road to the Cross. It keeps the order of the fourteen familiar stations, but suggests texts to accompany each one, also taken from St John's Gospel.

To some, these Roads to the Cross may seem too long, and the texts too full. When a shorter course is needed, for example when elderly people or even children are involved, there is nothing to prevent a selection of stations being used, chosen according to circumstances.

The passages from the Gospels are given in the translation of the Jerusalem Bible.

Marc Joulin

Introduction

In its present form – a communal or personal meditation on the passion in fourteen stages or 'stations' – the 'way of the cross' has become a devotional exercise which has been traditional in catholic practice since the Renaissance. But the original inspiration is as old as Christianity itself: did not Luke invite us to follow Jesus in carrying his cross, like Simon of Cyrene?

During the fifteenth century, the practice of making 'spiritual pilgrimages', which allowed those who could not go in person to the holy places to travel with Jesus in spirit (and to some degree in body, through movement) on his last journey, spread to the West. At that time there was a great variety in the number, the choice and the order of the 'stations'. It was not until the eighteenth century that the fourteen stations we know today gradually emerged, and the devotional practice established itself during the nineteenth century.

The fourteen stations in current use have the disadvantage of including incidents which are taken not from the Gospels but from pious legends (for example, Veronica's handkerchief, the three falls), of mixing up the four Gospel narratives, and of being excessively 'mournful'. They concentrate exclusively on the sufferings and death of Christ. Compare them, for example, with a twelfth-century stained glass window in Chartres cathedral, called 'The Window of the Passion'. This begins with the transfiguration and ends with the Risen Christ breaking bread with the disciples at Emmaus. Of the fourteen stations depicted in this window, there are only five which are centred on the actual passion. Five are on the resurrection.

In a small booklet which is now out of print, Fr Roguet had the idea of working out four Roads to the Cross according to the four Gospels. I have followed his idea, and often the choice of stations which he made.

Each of these Roads to the Cross uses the most characteristic scenes from each Gospel and especially those incidents which are unique to it (indicated in the following pages by an asterisk *). The title of each station tries to capture its essential aspect.

I suggest that you begin by reading the episode of the transfiguration in the Gospels of Matthew, Mark and Luke, and its equivalent in John. This has two advantages. The passion does not stand by itself, isolated from other events; it is placed firmly in the context of Jesus' life by this incident which heralds it. And, moreover, in this way we are led to meditate on the passion in the light of Jesus' glorification, of which the transfiguration is itself an anticipation. Each Road finishes with a final meditation on the resurrection, which gives meaning to Jesus' life. In Churches where the exercise is undertaken by a group, these two passages can be read from the altar.

At the end of the book there is a list of the stations, with their titles, so that the user can easily compare the various Roads to the Cross.

I have not tried to offer a ready-made way of the cross; each individual and each group must use the meditation in the way best suited to their own needs. I have only sketched out the framework for the meditation: a few notes drawing attention to significant points in the text, and some suggestions for prayer.

After announcing the title of each station, the leader could point out a few details in the passage which is to be read to allow those who are listening to gain as much as possible from it. I have done no more than sketch the bare outlines here; the leader will be able to draw on them to make his own presentation according to the biblical knowledge and the particular concerns of those in his group.

Some of the readings might appear to be a little lengthy, but experience shows that if a passage is read slowly and clearly, people do listen attentively.

After keeping silence for a time, the leader can gather up private prayer into a short and simple communal expression.

Is singing advisable? Experience again shows that often the concentrated impact of the Gospel passages makes any accompanying verses seem superfluous. But singing can also be a way of expressing communal prayer; so you could choose some well-known verses or one or two stanzas from a canticle, being careful to fit them in with the meaning of the episode which has just been used for meditation.

I want finally to reassure those who might be wondering about something which they wrongly take to be an innovation. Catholic canon law lays down that the way of the cross involves meditating on episodes of the passion (it does not state which), and in following a particular route marked out by fourteen wooden crosses (the moving on can be done by one person out of a group). The Roads to the Cross which I suggest here obey these rules implicitly.

One last thing. Anyone who reads these Roads to the Cross one after the other will sometimes find suggestions and remarks repeated. In order not to have any cross-references, which would make the book difficult to use, I have preferred to run the risk of repeating myself now and then from one to the other.

Etienne Charpentier

The Road to the Cross according to

St Matthew

Introduction: **The transfiguration: Jesus sees in advance the glory of the resurrection.**

17 ¹ Six days later, Jesus took with him Peter and James and his brother John and led them up a high mountain where they could be alone. ² There in their presence he was transfigured: his face shone like the sun and his clothes became as white as the light. ³ Suddenly Moses and Elijah appeared to them; they were talking with him. ⁴ Then Peter spoke to Jesus. 'Lord,' he said 'it is wonderful for us to be here; if you wish, I will make three tents here, one for you, one for Moses and one for Elijah.' ⁵ He was still speaking when suddenly a bright cloud covered them with shadow, and from the cloud there came a voice which said, 'This is my Son, the Beloved; he enjoys my favour. Listen to him.' ⁶ When they heard this, the disciples fell on their faces, overcome with fear. ⁷ But Jesus came up and touched them. 'Stand up,' he said 'do not be afraid.' ⁸ And when they raised their eyes they saw no one but only Jesus.

⁹ As they came down from the mountain Jesus gave them this order, 'Tell no one about the vision until the Son of Man has risen from the dead.'

The transfiguration takes place in Jesus' life towards the end of his ministry in Galilee, at a time when the crowds are walking out on him and the Jewish leaders are stepping up their pressure on him. Jesus realizes that if he upsets too many people, if he carries on in the same way, he risks a violent death, and to be faithful to what he has been sent to do, he deliberately takes that risk. So the Father allows him a foretaste of the glory he will achieve through the resurrection. And by clinging to this highlight in his life, Jesus finds the strength to go forward to his passion.

Jesus allows three disciples to glimpse something of this glory, and of the intimate conversation which he holds with Moses and Elijah, the two men who walked in the closest intimacy with God. So that they may follow their master to the cross, the Father reveals to the three disciples that Jesus is indeed his Son, his beloved, 'who enjoys my favour', adds Matthew. This realization strikes terror into the disciples. Jesus forbids them to say anything about what has been revealed to them until the time when he will be glorified beyond his death.

Lord Jesus, you were steadfast in what you had been sent to do, and accepted death.

As we follow you along the way of the cross, help us to find strength so that we, too, are steadfast in our daily work and as Christians in the service of God and our fellow men. May we hold fast in the midst of difficulties, suffering and uncertainties, inspired by the light of your resurrection.

1. The Jewish leaders and Judas surrender Jesus for the price of a slave.

26 ¹ Jesus had now finished all he wanted to say, and he told his disciples, ² 'It will be Passover, as you know, in two days' time, and the Son of Man will be handed over to be crucified.'

³ Then the chief priests and the elders of the people assembled in the palace of the high priest, whose name was Caiaphas, ⁴ and made plans to arrest Jesus by some trick and have him put to death. ⁵ They said, however, 'It must not be during the festivities; there must be no disturbance among the people.'

¹⁴ Then one of the Twelve, the man called Judas Iscariot, went to the chief priests ¹⁵ and said, 'What are you prepared to give me if I hand him over to you?' ¹⁶ They paid him thirty silver pieces, and from that moment he looked for an opportunity to betray him.

The passion is a scandal for the believer. If Jesus is truly the Messiah, the Christ, how could he be condemned to death by the Jewish leaders? From the very beginning of his narrative, Matthew tries to strengthen our faith, and has Jesus himself uncover the conspiracy woven around him. He therefore appears as the sovereign Lord who knows what is going to happen, and the chief priests can but carry out his will.

Moreover, in speaking of their conspiracy and their rallying against Jesus, Matthew uses the words which, in Psalm 2, denote the enemies of the Messiah. It is therefore a way of saying to us: Jesus is indeed the Messiah; the Jewish leaders are enemies of God and of his Messiah, but God will make him triumphant and will give him power over all nations, power heralded in this psalm.

Matthew is the only one to specify that Judas was paid thirty pieces of silver. In this connection he quotes the prophet Zechariah who, several centuries before Christ, demonstrated through an important parable that the people had rejected their God and to make fun of him had paid the paltry price of a slave for him. So the evangelist shows this prophecy fulfilled. In Jesus, it is God himself whom the people reject.

Lord Jesus, today as at other times everything goes against your being the Christ. You are still persecuted and broken in the persons of your disciples and of men of good will who fight for justice.

Help us to believe, in spite of everything, that you are the Lord who guides the outcome of things. Help us to believe that suffering and death can be the way to resurrection. Do not allow us in our fear to reject you as Judas did, preferring our own comfort and security to God's way and yours.

2. Jesus celebrates his last supper where he offers himself for the forgiveness of sins, while Judas betrays him.

26 ¹⁷ Now on the first day of Unleavened Bread the disciples came to Jesus to say, 'Where do you want us to make the preparations for you to eat the passover?' ¹⁸ 'Go to so-and-so in the city,' he replied 'and say to him, "The Master says: My time is near. It is at your house that I am

keeping Passover with my disciples." ' ⁱ⁹ The disciples did what Jesus told them and prepared the Passover.

²⁰ When evening came he was at table with the twelve disciples. ²¹ And while they were eating he said, 'I tell you solemnly, one of you is about to betray me.' ²² They were greatly distressed and started asking him in turn, 'Not I, Lord, surely?' ²³ He answered, 'Someone who has dipped his hand into the dish with me, will betray me. ²⁴ The Son of Man is going to his fate, as the scriptures say he will, but alas for that man by whom the Son of Man is betrayed! Better for that man if he had never been born!' ²⁵ Judas, who was to betray him, asked in his turn, 'Not I, Rabbi, surely?' 'They are your own words,' answered Jesus.

²⁶ Now as they were eating, Jesus took some bread, and when he had said the blessing he broke it and gave it to the disciples. 'Take it and eat,' he said; 'this is my body.' ²⁷ Then he took a cup, and when he had returned thanks he gave it to them. 'Drink all of you from this,' he said ²⁸ 'for this is my blood, the blood of the covenant, which is to be poured out for many for the forgiveness of sins. ²⁹ From now on, I tell you, I shall not drink wine until the day I drink the new wine with you in the kingdom of my Father.'

Jesus himself makes the preparations for his last supper. He is the Lord who controls what is happening. During the meal he offers bread and wine, his broken body and his blood, the true covenant between God and men. He sheds this blood for the forgiveness of sins.

At the heart of this narrative, Matthew puts Jesus' announcement of Judas' betrayal. In this way he is reminding his own community that no one should think himself incapable of betraying Jesus, even if he does share his meal.

Lord Jesus, we can scarcely recognize you in the bread and wine of our eucharists. Increase our faith.

We are often tempted to betray you, not perhaps by our words but more often by our life, by our attitude towards you and towards our fellow men for whom you died. Cherish our faith and our love for others. And if we have betrayed you, keep our hope alive. Remind us that you shed your blood for the forgiveness of sins.

3. On the way to Gethsemane, Jesus tells Peter that he will disown him.

> 26 ³⁰ After psalms had been sung they left for the Mount of Olives. ³¹ Then Jesus said to them, 'You will all lose faith in me this night, for the scripture says: I shall strike the shepherd and the sheep of the flock will be scattered, ³² but after my resurrection I shall go before you to Galilee.' ³³ At this, Peter said, 'Though all lose faith in you, I will never lose faith.' ³⁴ Jesus answered him, 'I tell you solemnly, this very night, before the cock crows, you will have disowned me three times.' ³⁵ Peter said to him, 'Even if I have to die with you, I will never disown you.' And all the disciples said the same.

Jesus is well aware that his life, his non-violence in the face of evil and his apparent helplessness in the face of death are difficult for his disciples to accept. He warns them: You might well be deeply offended because of me. And Peter protests: I will never be offended because of you!

Jesus knows that he is fulfilling the scriptures in which he reads God's plan; he knows that his disciples are going to scatter. But the resurrection will draw them together again.

Lord Jesus, how true it is that you are difficult to live by! Because you seem to be powerless in our world, because you tolerate the suffering of innocent people, the injustice of the powerful, the persecution of those who put themselves at the service of others, we are sometimes tempted to be offended or to forget you, if not to disown you.

Help us to believe, in spite of everything, in your resurrection and ours, and in God's victory over evil and death.

4. In Gethsemane, Jesus is afraid of death and seeks help from his disciples. But he accepts the will of the Father.

26 ³⁶ Then Jesus came with them to a small estate called Gethsemane; and he said to his disciples, 'Stay here while I go over there to pray.' ³⁷ He took Peter and the two sons of Zebedee with him. And sadness came over him, and great distress. ³⁸ Then he said to them, 'My soul is sorrowful to the point of death. Wait here and keep awake with me.' ³⁹ And going on a little further he fell on his face and prayed. 'My Father,' he said 'if it is possible, let this cup pass me by. Nevertheless, let it be as you, not I, would have it.' ⁴⁰ He came back to the disciples and found them sleeping, and he said to Peter, 'So you had not the strength to keep awake with me one hour? ⁴¹ You should be awake, and praying not to be put to the test. The spirit is willing, but the flesh is weak.' ⁴² Again, a second time, he went away and prayed: 'My Father,' he said 'if this cup cannot pass by without my drinking it, your will be done!' ⁴³ And he came back again and found them sleeping, their eyes were so heavy. ⁴⁴ Leaving them there, he went away again and prayed for the third time, repeating the same words. ⁴⁵ Then he came back to the disciples and said to them, 'You can sleep on now and take your rest. Now the hour has come when the Son of Man is to be betrayed into the hands of sinners. ⁴⁶ Get up! Let us go! My betrayer is already close at hand.'

In Gethsemane, Jesus shows himself to be fully human. He is afraid of suffering and death. Like everyone who suffers, he needs human beings near him. Three times during his narrative Matthew uses the moving words 'with me': 'Watch with me.' But Jesus is denied even this human comfort. His disciples are asleep!

The agony is Jesus' hour, the hour when he fulfils the will of the Father. And he comes to it sorrowfully.

The agony is a pattern for us, too, when we are tempted. Like Jesus, we must watch and pray.

Lord Jesus, you show yourself here to be fully human. Our griefs and fears are well known to you. Teach us to live through them with you. Help us never to refuse to be with you, who go on being in agony to the end of time in all your brothers who suffer and wait for your coming.

Help us to watch and pray with you in temptation. Guide us to do the will of the Father.

5. Jesus, when arrested, refuses to use his divine power.

26 ⁴⁷ He was still speaking when Judas, one of the Twelve, appeared, and with him a large number of men armed with swords and clubs, sent by the chief priests and elders of the people. ⁴⁸ Now the traitor had arranged a sign with them. 'The one I kiss,' he had said, 'he is the man. Take him in charge.' ⁴⁹ So he went straight up to Jesus and said, 'Greetings, Rabbi', and kissed him. ⁵⁰ Jesus said to him, 'My friend, do what you are here for.' Then they came forward, seized Jesus and took him in charge. ⁵¹ At that, one of the followers of Jesus grasped his sword and drew it; he struck out at the high priest's servant, and cut off his ear. ⁵² Jesus then said, 'Put your sword back, for all who draw the sword will die by the sword. ⁵³ Or do you think that I cannot appeal to my Father who would promptly send more than twelve legions of angels to my defence? ⁵⁴ But then, how would the scriptures be fulfilled that say this is the way it must be?' ⁵⁵ It was at this time that Jesus said to the crowds, 'Am I a brigand, that you had to set out to capture me with swords and clubs? I sat teaching in the Temple day after day and you never laid hands on me.' ⁵⁶ Now all this happened to fulfil the prophecies in scripture. Then all the disciples deserted him and ran away.

Jesus greets Judas and calls him 'friend'. He reminds the disciple who tries to defend him with a sword that the Father could send all his power to his aid. But Jesus wants to fulfil God's purpose as he has read it in the scriptures. And he tells it again to the crowds. He does not endure his passion; he takes it on through faithfulness to his Father.

Lord Jesus, when we are tempted to betray you, let us not be deaf to your voice calling us 'friend'.

When we have to come into conflict with others, or stand up to those who wish us ill, give us the strength to do it with love.

Help us to understand the scriptures and so remain steadfast to the will of the Father.

6. In front of the high priest, Jesus says who he is.

26 ⁵⁷ The men who had arrested Jesus led him off to Caiaphas the high priest, where the scribes and the elders were assembled. ⁵⁸ Peter followed him at a distance, and when he reached the high priest's palace, he went in and sat down with the attendants to see what the end would be.

⁵⁹ The chief priests and the whole Sanhedrin were looking for evidence against Jesus, however false, on which they might pass the death-sentence. ⁶⁰ But they could not find any, though several lying witnesses came forward. Eventually two stepped forward ⁶¹ and made a statement: 'This man said, "I have power to destroy the Temple of God and in three days build it up."' ⁶² The high priest then stood up and said to him, 'Have you no answer to that? What is this evidence these men are bringing against you?' ⁶³ But Jesus was silent. And the high priest said to him, 'I put you on oath by the living God to tell us if you are the Christ, the Son of God.' ⁶⁴ The words are your own,' answered Jesus. 'Moreover, I tell you that from this time onward you will see the Son of Man seated at the right hand of the Power and coming on the clouds of heaven.' ⁶⁵ At this, the high priest tore his clothes and said, 'He has blasphemed. What need of witnesses have we now? There! You have just heard the blasphemy. ⁶⁶ What is your opinion?' They answered, 'He deserves to die.'

⁶⁷ Then they spat in his face and hit him with their fists; others said as they struck him, ⁶⁸ 'Play the prophet, Christ! Who hit you then?'

With a gravity which indicates the importance of the reply, the high priest questions Jesus about his identity. Jesus announces that from this time onward the end of the age has begun, the time when he, the glorious Son of Man, proclaimed by the prophet Daniel, will come on the clouds of heaven, the time when, as Messiah, he will be enthroned as Lord of the world.

Coming as it does from a man already condemned to death, the assertion seems so ridiculous that they mock him and spit in his face.

Lord Jesus, the assertion that you are Lord of the world, the judge of the end of time coming to establish peace and justice, seems to us to be such a contradiction of what actually happens that we often find it difficult to believe.

Give us faith. And give us the strength to labour so that God's reign is brought about today, through us, here where we are.

7. Peter disowns his master.

26 ⁶⁹ Meanwhile Peter was sitting outside in the courtyard, and a servant-girl came up to him and said, 'You too were with Jesus the Galilean.' ⁷⁰ But he denied it in front of them all. 'I do not know what you are talking about,' he said. ⁷¹ When he went out to the gateway another servant-girl saw him and said to the people there, 'This man was with Jesus the Nazarene.' ⁷² And again, with an oath, he denied it, 'I do not know the man.' ⁷³ A little later the bystanders came up and said to Peter, 'You are one of them for sure! Why, your accent gives you away.' ⁷⁴ Then he started calling down curses on himself and swearing, 'I do not know the man.' At that moment the cock crew, ⁷⁵ and Peter remembered what Jesus had said: 'Before the cock crows you will have disowned me three times.' And he went outside and wept bitterly.

While Jesus, face to face with death, is courageously proclaiming who he is, Peter is disowning him in front of a servant.

'Lord, do not trust me because I am going to betray you,' said St Philip Neri. You know that we are going to betray you, and yet you are still willing to trust us.

May your word protect us from betraying you, and may it transform us if we should find ourselves disowning you.

*8. Judas despairs of Christ's forgiveness.

27 ¹ When morning came, all the chief priests and the elders of the people met in council to bring about the death of Jesus. ² They had him bound, and led him away to hand him over to Pilate, the governor.

³ When he found that Jesus had been condemned, Judas his betrayer was filled with remorse and took the thirty silver pieces back to the chief priests and elders. ⁴ 'I have sinned,' he said. 'I have betrayed innocent blood.' 'What is that to us?', they replied. 'That is your concern.' ⁵ And flinging down the silver pieces in the sanctuary he made off, and went and hanged himself. ⁶ The chief priests picked up the silver pieces and said, 'It is against the Law to put this into the treasury; it is blood-money.' ⁷ So they discussed the matter and bought the potter's field with it as a graveyard for foreigners, ⁸ and this is why the field is called the Field of Blood today. ⁹ The words of the prophet Jeremiah were then fulfilled: And they took the thirty silver pieces, the sum at which the precious One was priced by children of Israel, ¹⁰ and they gave them for the potter's field, just as the Lord directed me.

Judas did not know how to read in Christ's face the forgiveness he was offering him. In despair, he went and hanged himself.

In Judas' action of throwing the price of crime into the sanctuary, Matthew saw the fulfilment of the prophet's words: truly it was God who was rejected in Jesus.

Lord Jesus, you died for all men, and you showed forgiveness to Judas by calling him your friend. You keep hope alive in us when there is no longer any hope.

Even in the depths of our sin and hell, we know that it is your face that we meet, offering us your forgiveness, your friendship and the constant promise of a new life.

May we never insult you by despairing of your love.

9. In spite of his wife's intervention, Pilate condemns Jesus Christ and frees Jesus Barabbas.

27 ¹¹ Jesus, then, was brought before the governor, and the governor put to him this question, 'Are you the king of the Jews?' Jesus replied, 'It is you who say it.' ¹² But when he was accused by the chief priests and the elders he refused to answer at all. ¹³ Pilate then said to him, 'Do you not hear how many charges they have brought against you?' ¹⁴ But to the governor's complete amazement, he offered no reply to any of the charges.

¹⁵ At festival time it was the governor's practice to release a prisoner for the people, anyone they chose. ¹⁶ Now there was at that time a notorious prisoner whose name was Barabbas. ¹⁷ So when the crowd gathered, Pilate said to them, 'Which do you want me to release for you: Barabbas, or Jesus who is called Christ?' ¹⁸ For Pilate knew it was out of jealousy that they had handed him over.

¹⁹ Now as he was seated in the chair of judgment, his wife sent him a message: 'Have nothing to do with that man; I have been upset all day by a dream I had about him.'

²⁰ The chief priests and the elders, however, had persuaded the crowd to demand the release of Barabbas and the execution of Jesus. ²¹ So when the governor spoke and asked them, 'Which of the two do you want me to release for you?' they said, 'Barabbas'. ²² 'But in that case,' Pilate said to them, 'what am I to do with Jesus who is called Christ?' They all said, 'Let him be crucified!' ²³ 'Why?' he asked: 'What harm has he done?' But they shouted all the louder, 'Let him be crucified!' ²⁴ Then Pilate saw that he was making no impression, that in fact a riot was imminent. So he took some water, washed his hands in front of the crowd and said, 'I am innocent of this man's blood. It is your concern.' ²⁵ And the people, to a man, shouted back, 'His blood be on us and on our children!' ²⁶ Then he released Barabbas for them. He ordered Jesus to be first scourged and then handed over to be crucified.

Pilate's wife pleads with her husband to free Jesus; in this way

Matthew shows that even the Romans realize that Jesus is innocent. But, urged on by the chief priests, the crowd chooses Barabbas the public enemy rather than Jesus the Christ. In an action which has become proverbial, Pilate 'washes his hands' of the affair and the people shout that they will assume responsibility for this death: 'His blood be on us . . .' We are there at a turning point in the history of salvation. From this time forward, to attain salvation all people, Jews and Gentiles, have to enter into a covenant sealed by the blood of Christ.

Lord Jesus, your blood is on us and on all men, not to accuse us but to wash us clean from our sins and to seal the covenant for all time between us and your Father.

Never allow us to wash our hands of wretchedness and injustice. Let us be with you on the side of the poor and the oppressed.

10. Jesus is crowned with thorns and given a mock sceptre.

27 ²⁷ The governor's soldiers took Jesus with them into the Praetorium and collected the whole cohort round him. ²⁸ Then they stripped him and made him wear a scarlet cloak, ²⁹ and having twisted some thorns into a crown they put this on his head and placed a reed in his right hand. To make fun of him they knelt to him saying, 'Hail, king of the Jews!' ³⁰ And they spat on him and took the reed and struck him on the head with it. ³¹ And when they had finished making fun of him, they took off the cloak and dressed him in his own clothes and led him away to crucify him.

Clothed in a Roman soldier's red cloak, with a crown of thorns on his head, Jesus is given a reed as a royal sceptre. And he is ridiculed.

Lord Jesus, we recognize your royal power over us and over the world. But we know that you have no wish to reign as all-powerful Lord. Your sceptre is only a fragile reed! Protect your Church from wanting to dominate the world and imposing its wishes on it. Forgive it for all the persecutions of the past, and the persecutions going on today, and teach it humility. Take from our hearts the desire to impose our choices and preferences on others. Teach us, as St Paul says, that 'it is in our weakness that we are strong'.

11. The Righteous Man suffers and is crucified.

27 ³² On their way out, they came across a man from Cyrene, Simon by name, and enlisted him to carry his cross. ³³ When they had reached a place called Golgotha, that is, the place of the skull, ³⁴ they gave him wine to drink mixed with gall, which he tasted but refused to drink. ³⁵ When they had finished crucifying him they shared out his clothing by casting lots, ³⁶ and then sat down and stayed there keeping guard over him.

³⁷ Above his head was placed the charge against him; it read: 'This is Jesus, the King of the Jews.' ³⁸ At the same time two robbers were crucified with him, one on the right and one on the left.

³⁹ The passers-by jeered at him; they shook their heads ⁴⁰ and said, 'So you would destroy the Temple and rebuild it in three days! Then save yourself! If you are God's son, come down from the cross!' ⁴¹ The chief priests with the scribes and elders mocked him in the same way. ⁴² 'He saved others,' they said; 'he cannot save himself. He is the king of Israel; let him come down from the cross now, and we will believe in him. ⁴³ He puts his trust in God; now let God rescue him if he wants him. For he did say, "I am the son of God." ' ⁴⁴ Even the robbers who were crucified with him taunted him in the same way.

To describe Jesus' crucifixion, Matthew makes use of particular psalms which recall the persecution of the righteous man. In this way he proclaims that Jesus' fate gathers into itself the sufferings and death of all those who are unjustly persecuted.

Lord Jesus, you experience not only your own suffering and your own death, but also the suffering and death of all those in pain or being persecuted. May all their suffering and death find a meaning in yours.

You did not come to deliver us from our human lot. Teach us to live it, with you, as an offering.

*12. Jesus' death on the cross signals the new age.

27 ⁴⁵ From the sixth hour there was darkness over all the land until the ninth hour. ⁴⁶ And about the ninth hour, Jesus cried out in a loud voice, 'Eli, Eli, lama sabachthani?', that is, 'My God, my God, why have you deserted me?' ⁴⁷ When some of those who stood there heard this, they said, 'The man is calling on Elijah,' ⁴⁸ and one of them quickly ran to get a sponge which he dipped in vinegar and, putting it on a reed, gave it him to drink. ⁴⁹ 'Wait!' said the rest of them 'and see if Elijah will come to save him.' ⁵⁰ But Jesus, again crying out in a loud voice, yielded up his spirit.

⁵¹ At that, the veil of the Temple was torn in two from top to bottom; the earth quaked; the rocks were split; ⁵² the tombs opened and the bodies of many holy men rose from the dead, ⁵³ and these, after his resurrection, came out of the tombs, entered the Holy City and appeared to a number of people. ⁵⁴ Meanwhile the centurion, together with the others guarding Jesus, had seen the earthquake and all that was taking place, and they were terrified and said, 'In truth this was a son of God.'

Matthew records only one cry of Jesus from the cross, one which expresses his terrible loneliness. It seems that even the Father abandons him. And he dies with a loud cry.

But this death is the beginning of a new age, the last age. The earthquake, or tremor, which accompanies his death is the omen that Jesus had already said would signal the end of the world. With his eyes of faith, Matthew sees the saints rising from the dead and entering heaven. And through his faith, the Roman soldier enters the kingdom of God by recognizing the Son of God in Jesus.

Lord Jesus, you wanted to experience for yourself what it is like to die, even the grief of seeming to be abandoned by the Father. Out of your loneliness, let us draw the strength to believe that the Father is always with us, even when everything hides his presence from us.

Show us that the new age has really begun with your death and resurrection. And show us how to live now as citizens of the kingdom of Heaven.

13. The chief priests put a guard on Jesus' tomb.

27 ⁵⁵ And many women were there, watching from a distance, the same women who had followed Jesus from Galilee and looked after him. ⁵⁶ Among them were Mary of Magdala, Mary the mother of James and Joseph, and the mother of Zebedee's sons.

⁵⁷ When it was evening, there came a rich man of Arimathaea, called Joseph, who had himself become a disciple of Jesus. ⁵⁸ This man went to Pilate and asked for the body of Jesus. Pilate thereupon ordered it to be handed over. ⁵⁹ So Joseph took the body, wrapped it in a clean shroud ⁶⁰ and put it in his own new tomb which he had hewn out of the rock. He then rolled a large stone across the entrance of the tomb and went away. ⁶¹ Now Mary of Magdala and the other Mary were there, sitting opposite the sepulchre.

⁶² Next day, that is, when Preparation Day was over, the chief priests and the Pharisees went in a body to Pilate ⁶³ and said to him, 'Your Excellency, we recall that this impostor said, while he was still alive, "After three days I shall rise again." ⁶⁴ Therefore give the order to have the sepulchre kept secure until the third day, for fear his disciples come and steal him away and tell the people, "He has risen from the dead." This last piece of fraud would be worse than what went before.' ⁶⁵ You may have your guard,' said Pilate to them. 'Go and make all as secure as you know how.' ⁶⁶ So they went and made the sepulchre secure, putting seals on the stone and mounting a guard.

Jesus is buried by Joseph of Arimathaea, one of his disciples. Matthew emphasizes two details in his narrative; the body is wrapped in a *clean* shroud and laid in a *new* tomb. Even Jesus' sepulchre shows that a new age is beginning.

The chief priests come to seal the tomb. They secure permission from Pilate to have a guard placed there. By including these details, Matthew stresses the power of the Risen Lord who makes light of these pathetic precautions.

But above all, the chief priests themselves recall that Jesus had announced his resurrection and they proclaim in advance the message of the first Christians.

Lord Jesus, many people – ourselves among them, sometimes – wish they could shut you up in death, and seal the door of your tomb so that you could not come and disturb us any more. Show us that our precautions are pathetic, and that you are stronger than death and our fears.

Even in front of your tomb and in the face of your seeming absence in our world, help us to believe in the power of your resurrection.

*14. The open tomb brings in the new age.

28 ¹ After the sabbath, and towards dawn on the first day of the week, Mary of Magdala and the other Mary went to visit the sepulchre. ² And all at once there was a violent earthquake, for the angel of the Lord, descending from heaven, came and rolled away the stone and sat on it. ³ His face was like lightning, his robe white as snow. ⁴ The guards were so shaken, so frightened of him, that they were like dead men. ⁵ But the angel spoke; and he said to the women, 'There is no need for you to be afraid. I know you are looking for Jesus, who was crucified. ⁶ He is not here, for he has risen, as he said he would. Come and see the place where he lay, ⁷ then go quickly and tell his disciples, "He has risen from the dead and now he is going before you to Galilee; it is there you will see him." Now I have told you.' ⁸ Filled with awe and great joy the women came quickly away from the tomb and ran to tell the disciples.

⁹ And there, coming to meet them, was Jesus. 'Greetings,' he said. And the women came up to him and, falling down before him, clasped his feet. ¹⁰ Then Jesus said to them, 'Do not be afraid; go and tell my brothers that they must leave for Galilee; they will see me there.'

The earthquake which had already made itself felt at the time of

Jesus' death, the earth tremor signalling the end of an age, happens again. It opens the tomb and makes the guards shake with fear. And God tells the women who have come to pay their respects that Jesus is risen from the dead. Jesus himself appears to them and commissions them to be his first messengers.

Lord Jesus, your tomb is opened and from now on everything is possible; the new age has come, your Father's kingdom is beginning.

May our faith in your resurrection never falter. When we stand in front of the graves of those we love, help us to believe that on that Easter morning, God opened them all. Show us that our death is our entrance to life eternal in your kingdom.

Conclusion: The glorified Jesus sends his disciples into all the world.

28 ¹⁶ Meanwhile the eleven disciples set out for Galilee, to the mountain where Jesus had arranged to meet them. ¹⁷ When they saw him they fell down before him, though some hesitated. ¹⁸ Jesus came up and spoke to them. He said, 'All authority in heaven and on earth has been given to me. ¹⁹ Go, therefore, make disciples of all the nations; baptize them in the name of the Father and of the Son and of the Holy Spirit, ²⁰ and teach them to observe all the commands I gave you. And know that I am with you always; yes, to the end of time.'

Jesus is exalted, caught up into his Father's glory. It is in the majesty of the glorious Son of Man that he appears to his disciples. He comes to them with power over all the world.

God's final victory is already established. His Church has only to bring it to fruition by making the power of the Risen Christ known throughout the world.

And the only assurance which the disciples have in their huge and impossible task is of knowing that Jesus is with them, that he is Emmanuel, 'God-with-us'.

Lord Jesus, it is often difficult for us to believe that you have accomplished everything by your resurrection and that you have truly brought about your

Father's eternal kingdom, when everything seems so much to contradict this faith. Help us to believe.

You have entrusted to us, who are your Church, the task of spreading the news of your victory over evil and death throughout the whole world, beginning with the place where we live. By its loyalty to your teaching, by its diligent observation of the sacraments, by its faith in God, by its love for you and its obedience to the Holy Spirit, may your Church be in the world a true sign of your living presence.

The Road to the Cross according to

St Mark

Introduction: **Through the transfiguration, God gives Jesus the assurance of his love.**

9 ² Six days later, Jesus took with him Peter and James and John and led them up a high mountain where they could be alone by themselves. There in their presence he was transfigured: ³ his clothes became dazzlingly white, whiter than any earthly bleacher could make them. ⁴ Elijah appeared to them with Moses; and they were talking with Jesus. ⁵ Then Peter spoke to Jesus: 'Rabbi,' he said 'it is wonderful for us to be here; so let us make three tents, one for you, one for Moses and one for Elijah.' ⁶ He did not know what to say: they were so frightened. ⁷ And a cloud came, covering them in shadow; and there came a voice from the cloud, 'This is my Son, the Beloved. Listen to him.' ⁸ Then suddenly, when they looked round, they saw no one with them any more but only Jesus.

⁹ As they came down from the mountain he warned them to tell no one what they had seen, until after the Son of Man had risen from the dead.

Jesus has just told his disciples that the Son of Man is destined to suffer grievously, to be rejected by the elders and the chief priests and the scribes, and even be put to death. The transfiguration comes as God's answer to the terrible forebodings of the one whom he calls his beloved Son. The presence of Moses and Elijah, who symbolize the Law and the prophets, show Jesus to be the heir of the old covenant. The new covenant will be sealed with his blood, but after his resurrection he will enter into eternal glory, a glory in which all his people will share. The disciples do not understand, and wonder what 'rising from the dead' could mean.

Lord Jesus, for you the glory of your transfiguration was just a bright light along the pathway of dissension and death. But you stayed faithful to your mission to the end.

Help us to trust you even when we do not understand and suffer because of it. Keep us at one with all our fellow men. Maintain in us the hope of the resurrection, when we shall gather together and see you transfigured by the glory of the Father.

1. The chief priests have decided to put Jesus to death. A woman anticipates his burial by pouring ointment over his head.

14 ¹ It was two days before the Passover and the feast of Unleavened Bread, and the chief priests and the scribes were looking for a way to arrest Jesus by some trick and have him put to death. ² For they said, 'It must not be during the festivities, or there will be a disturbance among the people.'

³ Jesus was at Bethany in the house of Simon the leper; he was at dinner when a woman came in with an alabaster jar of very costly ointment, pure nard. She broke the jar and poured the ointment on his head. ⁴ Some who were there said to one another indignantly, 'Why this waste of ointment? ⁵ Ointment like this could have been sold for over three hundred denarii and the money given to the poor'; and they were angry with her. ⁶ But Jesus said, 'Leave her alone. Why are you upsetting her? What she has done for me is one of the good works. ⁷ You have the poor with you always, and you can be kind to them whenever you wish, but you will not always have me. ⁸ She has done what was in her power to do: she has anointed my body beforehand for its burial. ⁹ I tell you solemnly, wherever throughout all the world the Good News is proclaimed, what she has done will be told also, in remembrance of her.'

The decision is reached even before the trial takes place. The chief priests want Jesus put to death.

The woman who pours ointment over his head is certainly only intending to do him honour. Jesus sees in her action an anticipation of the burial rites which the women will not have time to perform. So he knows that his death is near, and he accepts it with his eyes open. But he also knows that this death is the prelude to the resurrection, that it is the Good News, the Gospel which will be proclaimed throughout the world.

Lord Jesus, in walking with you along the way of the cross, we are proclaiming the Good News. By your death, you give us life.
Give us the wisdom, like this woman, to express our love by our actions and in our lives. Let us be unselfish in our actions. You will be able to see the deeper meaning in them that we often cannot.
Show us how to tell the poor who surround us what you have done for them, as for us.

2. While Judas is betraying him, Jesus makes preparations for his last supper.

14 ¹⁰ Judas Iscariot, one of the Twelve, approached the chief priests with an offer to hand Jesus over to them. ¹¹ They were delighted to hear it, and promised to give him money; and he looked for a way of betraying him when the opportunity should occur.
¹² On the first day of Unleavened Bread, when the Passover lamb was sacrificed, his disciples said to him, 'Where do you want us to go and make the preparations for you to eat the passover?' ¹³ So he sent two of his disciples, saying to them, 'Go into the city and you will meet a man carrying a pitcher of water. Follow him, ¹⁴ and say to the owner of the house which he enters, "The Master says: Where is my dining room in which I can eat the passover with my disciples?" ¹⁵ He will show you a large upper room furnished with couches, all prepared. Make the preparations for us there.' ¹⁶ The disciples set out and went to the city and found everything as he had told them, and prepared the Passover.

Judas' betrayal, the bargain struck with the chief priests – all that is told in a few brief words like the entry in a diary. The brusqueness of the information throws its enormity into relief.

During this time Jesus is calmly making preparations for his last supper. He knows where he is going and what he wants.

And so two projects are set on a collision course. It seems that death will win. But in the end it is life which will triumph.

Lord, Jesus, the Gospel reports the decision to put you to death in the same curt and terse way as our papers report the news: '5000 people have "disappeared" in Argentina' or 'Thousands of children die through famine in Africa'. Evil pursues its course in the world and your passion goes on.

Do not let us remain indifferent. Show us how to help our fellow men. And give us strength to believe that you control all that happens and that your life will triumph; that in the end, out of so much suffering will come happiness and life.

3. Jesus gives himself to the disciples in his last supper; one of them betrays him and another will deny him.

14 ¹⁷ When evening came he arrived with the Twelve. ¹⁸ And while they were at table eating, Jesus said, 'I tell you solemnly, one of you is about to betray me, one of you eating with me.' ¹⁹ They were distressed and asked him, one after another, 'Not I, surely?' ²⁰ He said to them, 'It is one of the Twelve, one who is dipping into the same dish with me. ²¹ Yes, the Son of Man is going to his fate, as the scriptures say he will, but alas for that man by whom the Son of Man is betrayed! Better for that man if he had never been born!'

²² And as they were eating he took some bread, and when he had said the blessing he broke it and gave it to them. 'Take it,' he said 'this is my body.' ²³ Then he took a cup, and when he had returned thanks he gave it to them, and all drank from it, ²⁴ and he said to them, 'This is my blood, the blood of the covenant, which is to be poured out for many. ²⁵ I tell you solemnly, I shall not drink any more wine until the day I drink the new wine in the kingdom of God.'

The contrast is striking. In the gift of bread and wine, Jesus gives us his whole being, body and blood. But the narrative is framed by the story of Judas' betrayal and the prediction of Peter's denial! Jesus' reproach of Judas is not a curse, but a sad statement of fact. And the question which the disciples put to Jesus – 'Is it I who will betray you?' – shows quite clearly that not one of them is sure of himself, that any one of them might have done it.

Lord Jesus, is it I who will betray you? . . . Like the disciples, we are sure of neither our faith nor our love. Our security does not depend on our always fragile love, but on your own, which is ever-steadfast.

You show us this complete love when you give yourself to us in the last supper. Strengthen our faith in your presence when you break the bread for us in our eucharists. May they nourish in us a strong and real love towards you and towards our fellow men.

4. Jesus declares that Peter will disown him.

14 ²⁶ After psalms had been sung they left for the Mount of Olives. ²⁷ And Jesus said to them, 'You will all lose faith, for the scripture says: I shall strike the shepherd and the sheep will be scattered; ²⁸ however after my resurrection I shall go before you to Galilee.' ²⁹ Peter said, 'Even if all lose faith, I will not.' ³⁰ And Jesus said to him, 'I tell you solemnly, this day, this very night, before the cock crows twice, you will have disowned me three times.' ³¹ But he repeated still more earnestly, 'If I have to die with you, I will never disown you.' And they all said the same.

Jesus has no illusions. He knows that our faith is frail. He knows that Peter is going to disown him and that all the disciples will run away. But he speaks of his resurrection, when he will gather them together again in Galilee.

Lord Jesus, keep us from being over-confident, from believing that we are more steadfast in faith than others. We, too, can disown you!

Tirelessly you go before us on the path to unity. You alone, the Risen Lord, can draw us together. Do not allow us, your disciples – Catholic, Protestant, Orthodox – to become entrenched in our convictions, but let us be capable of recognizing our failures and always be moving towards you, who carry us with you.

5. Jesus suffers agony in Gethsemane.

14 ³² They came to a small estate called Gethsemane, and Jesus said to his disciples, 'Stay here while I pray.' ³³ Then he took Peter and James and John with him. And a sudden fear came over him, and great distress. ³⁴ And he said to them, 'My soul is sorrowful to the point of death. Wait here, and keep awake.' ³⁵ And going on a little further he threw himself on the ground and prayed that, if it were possible, this hour might pass him by. ³⁶ 'Abba (Father)!' he said 'Everything is possible for you. Take this cup away from me. But let it be as you, not I, would have it.' ³⁷ He came back and found them sleeping, and he said to Peter, 'Simon, are you asleep? Had you not the strength to keep awake one hour? ³⁸ You should be awake, and praying not to be put to the test. The spirit is willing, but the flesh is weak.' ³⁹ Again he went away and prayed, saying the same words. ⁴⁰ And once more he came back and found them sleeping, their eyes were so heavy; and they could find no answer for him. ⁴¹ He came back a third time and said to them, 'You can sleep on now and take your rest. It is all over. The hour has come. Now the Son of Man is to be betrayed into the hands of sinners. ⁴² Get up! Let us go! My betrayer is close at hand already.'

This is the moment in his life when Jesus seems the most human; in the face of suffering and death he is dismayed and frightened. His prayer to God is almost fierce: 'Everything is possible for you. Take this cup away from me!' But the intimacy of the affectionate name he calls him – 'Abba! Dear Father!' – brightens this tragic scene for a moment. And Jesus accepts the will of the Father.

For the three chosen disciples the mystery of Jesus' suffering is as incomprehensible as the mystery of his glory at the transfiguration. Again, 'they do not know how to answer him'.

Lord Jesus, you show yourself to be one of us. Our griefs and fears are familiar to you. Teach us to live through them with you. When we have to contend with suffering and death, give us the strength to do it in the knowledge that the all-loving Father is near us.

Enlighten our hearts so that we may in some measure come to understand your mystery. Do not let us leave you alone to endure the agony which you never cease to feel through the ages in all those who suffer and die.

6. Abandoned by everyone and arrested, alone Jesus undergoes his passion.

14 ⁴³ Even while he was still speaking, Judas, one of the Twelve, came up with a number of men armed with swords and clubs, sent by the chief priests and the scribes and the elders. ⁴⁴ Now the traitor had arranged a signal with them. 'The one I kiss,' he had said, 'he is the man. Take him in charge, and see he is well guarded when you lead him away.' ⁴⁵ So when the traitor came, he went straight up to Jesus and said, 'Rabbi!' and kissed him. ⁴⁶ The others seized him and took him in charge. ⁴⁷ Then one of the bystanders drew his sword and struck out at the high priest's servant, and cut off his ear.

⁴⁸ Then Jesus spoke. 'Am I a brigand,' he said 'that you had to set out to capture me with swords and clubs? ⁴⁹ I was among you teaching in the Temple day after day and you never laid hands on me. But this is to fulfil the scriptures.' ⁵⁰ And they all deserted him and ran away. ⁵¹ A young man who followed him had nothing on but a linen cloth. They caught hold of him, ⁵² but he left the cloth in their hands and ran away naked.

More than the others, Mark was aware of Christ's loneliness during his passion. His disciples have been with him until now, but one has already betrayed him, others sleep during his anguish and understand nothing of his mystery, Peter will soon betray him – and so everyone leaves him, even the last one, the young man who sought to follow him but who in the end ran away as well, naked. The word 'naked', which comes at the end of the story, underlines the tragedy of the passion. Jesus is utterly stripped of everything; naked, he is plunged into suffering and death.

When they were baptized, the first Christians stripped off their clothes and went naked into the water of baptism. As they listened to this narrative, they could recognize an allusion to their own baptism. Before being reclothed in Christ, they had first of all to be completely stripped of all the former person in them.

Lord Jesus, your passion is still going on today and we, your disciples, are still deaf to your mystery. We are still tempted to abandon you to suffering, both yours and that of our fellow men.
 Grant that we may live out our baptism and, stripped of all that is sinful, be restored to our true selves again and live for evermore in you and with you. And let us always live faithful to your love.

7. In front of the high priest, Jesus proclaims who he is.

14 ⁵³ They led Jesus off to the high priest; and all the chief priests and the elders and the scribes assembled there. ⁵⁴ Peter had followed him at a distance, right into the high priest's palace, and was sitting with the attendants warming himself at the fire.
 ⁵⁵ The chief priests and the whole Sanhedrin were looking for evidence against Jesus on which they might pass the death-sentence. But they could not find any. ⁵⁶ Several, indeed, brought false evidence against him, but their evidence was conflicting. ⁵⁷ Some stood up and submitted this false evidence against him. ⁵⁸ 'We heard him say, "I am going to destroy this Temple made by human hands, and in three days build another, not made by human hands." ' ⁵⁹ But even on this point their evidence was conflicting. ⁶⁰ The high priest then stood up before the whole assembly and put this question to Jesus. 'Have you no answer to that? What is this evidence these men are bringing against you?' ⁶¹ But he was silent and made no answer at all. The high priest put a second question to him. 'Are you the Christ,' he said, 'the Son of the Blessed One?' ⁶² 'I am,' said Jesus, 'and you will see the Son of Man seated at the right hand of the Power and coming with the clouds of heaven.' ⁶³ The high priest tore his robes. 'What need of witnesses have we now?' he said. ⁶⁴ 'You heard the blasphemy. What is your finding?' And they all gave their verdict: he deserved to die.

⁶⁵ Some of them started spitting at him and, blindfolding him, began hitting him with their fists and shouting, 'Play the prophet!' And the attendants rained blows on him.

The matter is already settled but, in order to maintain a semblance of legality, the chief priests and the whole Sanhedrin look for evidence against Jesus. They do not find any, and what is offered is false. Jesus is innocent.

Mark makes much of the evidence about the Temple. The Christian who hears it thinks of the true Temple which is Jesus' body. The place where God truly comes to meet man is in his mortal body, 'made by human hands' and fashioned from Mary's flesh. But so that everyone – Jews and Gentiles – can meet him there, until the end of the world, this body, this Temple, has to be rebuilt not with human hands but by the hand of God himself, as a body made spiritual by the resurrection.

According to Mark's Gospel, right up to that moment Jesus has always refused to say who he is; he is fearful of being misunderstood, of being taken for a glorious Messiah, a political figure, or a warrior. Now that he is condemned to death, and appears as the suffering servant announced by the prophet Isaiah, there is no longer any risk of being mistaken and he consents to reveal the truth. In answer to the high priest's question, he reveals himself as the Son of Man proclaimed by Daniel, coming on the clouds of heaven as the Messiah to be enthroned as Lord over the world.

This assertion seems so blasphemous coming from a man already condemned to death that the people spit in his face and the guards strike him viciously.

Lord Jesus, your risen body, transfigured by the Holy Spirit on Easter morning, is from that time forward the place where God meets us. We receive your risen body in the eucharist, we touch it in your disciples.

You are the Lord of the world. You have conquered evil, injustice and death. But what we see going on in the world often makes this difficult for us to believe. Give us faith, and strengthen us to work for the coming of your kingdom on earth.

8. Peter disowns his master.

14 ⁶⁶ While Peter was down below in the courtyard, one of the high priest's servant-girls came up. ⁶⁷ She saw Peter warming himself there, stared at him and said, 'You too were with Jesus, the man from Nazareth.' ⁶⁸ But he denied it. 'I do not know, I do not understand, what you are talking about,' he said. And he went out into the forecourt. ⁶⁹ The servant-girl saw him and again started telling the bystanders, 'This fellow is one of them.' ⁷⁰ But again he denied it. A little later the bystanders themselves said to Peter, 'You are one of them for sure! Why, you are a Galilean.' ⁷¹ But he started calling down curses on himself and swearing, 'I do not know the man you speak of.' ⁷² At that moment the cock crew for the second time, and Peter recalled how Jesus had said to him, 'Before the cock crows twice, you will have disowned me three times.' And he burst into tears.

Jesus' loneliness increases. Peter has followed him to the house of the high priest but only, in the end, to say that he does not know him . . .

Lord Jesus, in what we speak and what we do, we are always ready to abandon you and say that we do not know you.

Do not let us leave you alone, you and all the deprived and deserted people who are your presence among us. And if by chance we do, may your mercy change our hearts and bring us back to you.

9. Jesus, the king of the Jews, is rejected by the Jews and condemned by Pilate.

15 ¹ First thing in the morning, the chief priests together with the elders and scribes, in short the whole Sanhedrin, had their plan ready. They had Jesus bound and took him away and handed him over to Pilate.

² Pilate questioned him, 'Are you the king of the Jews?' 'It is you who say it,' he answered. ³ And the chief priests

brought many accusations against him. ⁴ Pilate questioned him again. 'Have you no reply at all? See how many accusations they are bringing against you!' ⁵ But, to Pilate's amazement, Jesus made no further reply.

⁶ At festival time Pilate used to release a prisoner for them, anyone they asked for. ⁷ Now a man called Barabbas was then in prison with the rioters who had committed murder during the uprising. ⁸ When the crowd went up and began to ask Pilate the customary favour, ⁹ Pilate answered them, 'Do you want me to release for you the king of the Jews?' ¹⁰ For he realized it was out of jealousy that the chief priests had handed Jesus over. ¹¹ The chief priests, however, had incited the crowd to demand that he should release Barabbas for them instead. ¹² Then Pilate spoke again. 'But in that case,' he said to them, 'what am I to do with the man you call king of the Jews?' ¹³ They shouted back, 'Crucify him!' ¹⁴ 'Why?' Pilate asked them. 'What harm has he done?' But they shouted all the louder, 'Crucify him!' ¹⁵ So Pilate, anxious to placate the crowd, released Barabbas for them and, having ordered Jesus to be scourged, handed him over to be crucified.

Throughout his Gospel, Mark makes us aware of the tragedy whose threads are being drawn together. The Jewish officials in Jerusalem had a pre-conceived idea of the Messiah, the king they were awaiting. Jesus announces that he is this Messiah, this king, but that he is so in a different way.

The conflict becomes so fierce that someone has to die. Either the Jewish officials give up the idea they have of the Messiah and listen to Jesus, or they become further entrenched in their prejudice and Jesus will have to die.

And so to the climax of the tragedy. The chief priests send Jesus in chains to the Roman governor Pilate for him to be executed. Three times, Pilate ironically proclaims Jesus to be 'king of the Jews'. But the religious leaders will not budge from their opinion and demand his death.

Jesus himself says nothing. His silence impresses even Pilate. Jesus has said who he is – the Messiah, the king of Israel. It only remains for him to show, by his life and death, that he is not a triumphant Messiah. He has not come to conquer evil outwardly with weapons, but inwardly, through suffering.

Lord Jesus, the tragedy goes on. Like the Jewish officials then, we are always inclined to be obstinate in our opinions; we cling to our all-too-human views of politics, society, the family, religion, our habit of reducing Christianity to squabbles between 'conservatives' and 'progressives'. And when we get an idea into our heads that we are convinced is right, we turn into persecutors and seek to obliterate our opponents.

Show us how to be tolerant. Help us sometimes to put our own considerations aside and accept the other person. Teach us to open ourselves to you, and realize that you offer us more than we can ever dream of.

10. The Roman soldiers mock the king of the Jews.

15 ¹⁶ The soldiers led him away to the inner part of the palace, that is, the Praetorium, and called the whole cohort together. ¹⁷ They dressed him up in purple, twisted some thorns into a crown and put it on him. ¹⁸ And they began saluting him, 'Hail, king of the Jews!' ¹⁹ They struck his head with a reed and spat on him; and they went down on their knees to do him homage. ²⁰ And when they had finished making fun of him, they took off the purple and dressed him in his own clothes.

The Roman soldiers recognize Jesus as king, but only to laugh him to scorn. The crown is made of thorns, and they pay him mock homage.

Lord Jesus, you are king, but your crown is made of thorns. The guards surround you, but not to protect and honour you – they are there to kill you!

Do not let the Church be tempted to show any face to the world save that of your weakness. May it not look for wealth, honour, easy victories and the protection of the world's powers. But let it be truly a poor servant in the service of the most poor.

11. Simon of Cyrene is made to carry Jesus' cross.

15 20 They led him out to crucify him. 21 They enlisted a passer-by, Simon of Cyrene, father of Alexander and Rufus, who was coming in from the country, to carry his cross. 22 They brought Jesus to the place called Golgotha, which means the place of the skull.

Simon of Cyrene will undoubtedly have become a Christian. But there is nothing to indicate that at the time he was a follower of Jesus. He was 'pressed into service' for an ignominious job.

Lord Jesus, a curt order from the occupying armies forces Simon to carry your cross. Something at which he undoubtedly rebels inwardly makes him your follower. And so it is in following you along your way of grief that he becomes your disciple.

Often things happen to us which we won't accept, and which we fight against. But show us that it is at the very heart of these things we are able to find you.

12. The Messiah, the king of the Jews, is crucified.

15 23 They offered him wine mixed with myrrh, but he refused it. 24 Then they crucified him, and shared out his clothing, casting lots to decide what each should get. 25 It was the third hour when they crucified him. 26 The inscription giving the charge against him read: 'The King of the Jews'. 27 And they crucified two robbers with him, one on his right and one on his left.

29 The passers-by jeered at him; they shook their heads and said, 'Aha! So you would destroy the Temple and rebuild it in three days! 30 Then save yourself: come down from the cross!' 31 The chief priests and the scribes mocked him among themselves in the same way. 'He saved others,' they said, 'he cannot save himself. 32 Let the Christ, the king of Israel, come down from the cross now, for us to see it and believe.' Even those who were crucified with him taunted him.

Jesus is crucified between two robbers. Above the cross is the inscription: 'The King of the Jews'. The chief priests jeer and hail him as Messiah, and the passers-by remind him of what he had said about the Temple.

And so, at the very moment when Jesus is suspended between heaven and earth, all the reasons for which he allowed himself to be killed are thrown into his face. His loneliness becomes overwhelming. Even the robbers who are being crucified with him insult him.

But St Mark begins to celebrate the liturgy of Christ's death. He indicates the hours by giving them the names which they will carry in the Church's daily pattern of prayer – 'terce', 'sext', 'none', at the third, sixth and ninth hours. And so, throughout its history, the Church celebrates the passion to keep faith with its crucified Messiah.

Lord Jesus, it would be hypocritical for us to pray, to celebrate your passion, or follow you along the way of the cross, if we do not at the same time struggle to bring about the kingdom of God and put an end to evil, and suffering and death.

But our fight for mankind, and for peace and love on the earth, has no real meaning without prayer.

May our human deeds be purified in the crucible of the cross. And may the light of Easter shine on us every day.

13. In dying on the cross, Jesus opens the Temple to all people.

15 ³³ When the sixth hour came there was darkness over the whole land until the ninth hour. ³⁴ And at the ninth hour Jesus cried out in a loud voice, 'Eloi, Eloi, lama sabachthani?' which means, 'My God, my God, why have you deserted me?' ³⁵ When some of those who stood by heard this, they said, 'Listen, he is calling on Elijah.' ³⁶ Someone ran and soaked a sponge in vinegar and, putting it on a reed, gave it him to drink saying, 'Wait and see if Elijah will come to take him down.' ³⁷ But Jesus gave a loud cry and breathed his last. ³⁸ And the veil of the Temple was torn in two from top to bottom. ³⁹ The centurion, who was stand-

ing in front of him, had seen how he had died, and he said, 'In truth this man was a son of God.'

⁴⁰ There were some women watching from a distance. Among them were Mary of Magdala, Mary who was the mother of James the younger and Joset, and Salome. ⁴¹ These used to follow him and look after him when he was in Galilee. And there were many other women there who had come up to Jerusalem with him.

Jesus' loneliness becomes unbearable. Sext – the sixth hour – is the hour of darkness. None – the ninth hour – is the one of utter abandonment. Even the Father seems to have forgotten him. For a moment, Jesus breaks his silence to shout his grief aloud: 'My God, why have you deserted me?' 'My God'. Not the 'Abba, Father' of the agony in the garden.

Jesus dies, and the veil of the Temple is torn in two. The veil which had been hiding the presence of God is drawn back. When driving the stall holders from the Temple, Jesus had said: 'My house will be called the house of prayer for all people.' Now, Gentiles and Jews alike can approach God, because from now on the true Temple is the body of Christ broken on the cross, a body which is already made whole again, not by man's hands but through the power of the Holy Spirit. And it is a Gentile, the Roman centurion, who is the first to enter the true Temple in faith: 'In truth, this man was a Son of God.'

Lord Jesus, you have known the most bitter loneliness, when even the Father was hidden from you. Keep our faith alive during those times when we have to make choices, to fight, and to suffer alone. Inspire in us the certain knowledge that the Father is always with us, too, when everything hides his presence from us.

Our true Temple, the place where God makes himself known to all people is his risen Body, your Church. May all approach him there freely. Through the way we act and the love we show, may we Christians encourage them to come, by showing them that life and joy are to be found there.

14. Jesus is laid in the tomb.

15 ⁴² It was now evening, and since it was Preparation Day (that is, the vigil of the sabbath), ⁴³ there came Joseph of Arimathaea, a prominent member of the Council, who himself lived in the hope of seeing the kingdom of God, and he boldly went to Pilate and asked for the body of Jesus. ⁴⁴ Pilate, astonished that he should have died so soon, summoned the centurion and enquired if he was already dead. ⁴⁵ Having been assured of this by the centurion, he granted the corpse to Joseph ⁴⁶ who bought a shroud, took Jesus down from the cross, wrapped him in the shroud and laid him in a tomb which had been hewn out of the rock. He then rolled a stone against the entrance to the tomb. ⁴⁷ Mary of Magdala and Mary the mother of Joset were watching and took note of where he was laid.

Now that everything is over, the narrative loses its tragic tone. Jesus' loneliness comes to an end with the mockeries and cruelty. A prominent member of the Jewish Council does the last honours for him; the women who will be told the news of the resurrection are there. And the evening before the sabbath day, when God himself ceased his labours at the creation of the world, brings rest to Jesus. We are about to witness the new creation.

Lord Jesus, it is only too easy to pay our respects to the dead, when we have let them face death alone. Teach us to respect and help our fellow men while they are still alive.

But when we are brought face to face with the cold stone of the tomb – whether of people we love or of our own – show us that death is only a time of rest and that at the end of this painful journey you and a new creation await us.

Conclusion: Go and tell the world that he who was crucified is risen!

16 ¹ When the sabbath was over, Mary of Magdala, Mary the mother of James, and Salome, bought spices with which to go and anoint him. ² And very early in the morning on

the first day of the week they went to the tomb, just as the sun was rising.

³ They had been saying to one another, 'Who will roll away the stone for us from the entrance to the tomb?' ⁴ But when they looked they could see that the stone – which was very big – had already been rolled back. ⁵ On entering the tomb they saw a young man in a white robe seated on the right-hand side, and they were struck with amazement. ⁶ But he said to them, 'There is no need for alarm. You are looking for Jesus of Nazareth, who was crucified: he has risen, he is not here. See, here is the place where they laid him. ⁷ But you must go and tell his disciples and Peter, "He is going before you to Galilee; it is there you will see him, just as he told you." ' ⁸ And the women came out and ran away from the tomb because they were frightened out of their wits; and they said nothing to a soul, for they were afraid . . .

The night and the sabbath day – the Jewish religious festival – have given way to sunrise on the first day of the week. One world has passed away. We are about to enter a new age.

A young man, 'seated on the right-hand side', as Jesus is on the Father's right hand, and clothed in a white robe, as the newly baptized are when they come out of the font, tells the women of the joy of Easter: He who was crucified is risen!

Mark's Gospel originally ended with the message which the women have to pass on to Peter and the disciples: 'He is going before you to Galilee; it is there you will see him.' For Mark, Galilee is the land open to Gentiles; so it stands both for the whole world and for the whole of history. Mark teaches us that we do not need to see the Risen Lord in order to believe in the resurrection. It is enough for God to tell us. And he makes us realize that we will only see the Risen Lord when we have proclaimed him to all the corners of the world and to the end of time.

But the message is so world-shattering that the terrified women run away and say nothing.

Lord Jesus, help us to believe that you have risen, not by trying to prove the impossible but by having confidence in God's word.

We will see you when we have proclaimed you to all the nations. Let us not falter in this task, so that your day may come – the day when, with all your people drawn from the four corners of the world and from all the ages, we may see you and sing hymns to you eternally with the Father and the Holy Spirit.

The Road to the Cross according to

St Luke

Introduction: **In the transfiguration, the disciples see Jesus' glory.**

9 ²⁸ Now about eight days after this had been said, he took with him Peter and John and James and went up the mountain to pray. ²⁹ As he prayed, the aspect of his face was changed and his clothing became brilliant as lightning. ³⁰ Suddenly there were two men there talking to him; they were Moses and Elijah ³¹ appearing in glory, and they were speaking of his passing which he was to accomplish in Jerusalem. ³² Peter and his companions were heavy with sleep, but they kept awake and saw his glory and the two men standing with him. ³³ As these were leaving him, Peter said to Jesus, 'Master, it is wonderful for us to be here; so let us make three tents, one for you, one for Moses and one for Elijah'. – He did not know what he was saying. ³⁴ As he spoke, a cloud came and covered them with shadow; and when they went into the cloud the disciples were afraid. ³⁵ And a voice came from the cloud saying, 'This is my Son, the Chosen One. Listen to him.' ³⁶ And after the voice had spoken, Jesus was found alone. The disciples kept silence and, at that time, told no one what they had seen.

Jesus has gone away with his three chosen disciples to pray. He has just said to them: 'If anyone wants to be a follower of mine, let him take up his cross.' He is well aware that his enemies are lying in wait for him, and that every day he risks death. Besides, it is about his death that he is speaking with Moses and Elijah. So he asks his closest friends to seek strength with him in prayer. And God answers his prayer by revealing to them the glory of the One he calls his Son. This fleeting glory is only a foretaste of the eternal glory which the resurrection will bring.

Lord Jesus, you liked to go alone into the mountains to pray. And God answered your prayer by giving you the strength to accept your cross and face your passion.

Grant us light to see how to travel along life's road bearing its difficulties and discords. And let faith in your resurrection encourage us to follow you courageously. with love.

1. Jesus longs to eat the passover with his disciples.

22 ¹ The feast of Unleavened Bread, called the Passover, was now drawing near, ² and the chief priests and the scribes were looking for some way of doing away with him, because they mistrusted the people.

³ Then Satan entered into Judas, surnamed Iscariot, who was numbered among the Twelve. ⁴ He went to the chief priests and the officers of the guard to discuss a scheme for handing Jesus over to them. ⁵ They were delighted and agreed to give him money. ⁶ He accepted, and looked for an opportunity to betray him to them without the people knowing.

⁷ The day of Unleavened Bread came round, the day on which the passover ⁸ had to be sacrificed.
. . . .

¹⁴ When the hour came he took his place at table, and the apostles with him. ¹⁵ And he said to them, 'I have longed to eat this passover with you before I suffer; ¹⁶ because, I tell you, I shall not eat it again until it is fulfilled in the kingdom of God.'

¹⁷ Then, taking a cup, he gave thanks and said, 'Take this and share it among you, ¹⁸ because from now on, I tell you, I shall not drink wine until the kingdom of God comes.'

¹⁹ Then he took some bread, and when he had given thanks, broke it and gave it to them, saying, 'This is my body which will be given for you; do this as a memorial of me. ²⁰ He did the same with the cup after supper, and said, 'This cup is the new covenant in my blood which will be poured out for you.'

In Luke's narrative, the passion comes across as the decisive battle between Jesus and the forces of evil personified by Satan. He now enters into Judas and leads the attack by inspiring not only the traitor, but the chief priests and leaders of the people as well. But Jesus keeps calm. He transforms the Jewish passover into the eucharist. He knows that it will be his last meal among men before the kingdom of God is brought about. He offers himself as a martyr who gives his body and his life for his friends. And his blood seals a new covenant between God and his people.

Lord Jesus, evil's final assault, which started with your passion, continues throughout history, in the world and in us. But we believe that the kingdom of God has begun and that you live among us, through your body given for us and your blood shed for us.

May your eucharist be our strength and our support in the fight against evil, and in our quest for greater love and justice. May it draw us towards you, who are eternal life.

*2. After supper, Jesus gives his last commands to his disciples.

22 ²¹ 'And yet, here with me on the table is the hand of the man who betrays me. ²² The Son of Man does indeed go to his fate even as it has been decreed, but alas for that man by whom he is betrayed!' ²³ And they began to ask one another which of them it could be who was to do this thing.

²⁴ A dispute arose also between them about which should be reckoned the greatest, ²⁵ but he said to them, 'Among pagans it is the kings who lord it over them, and those who have authority over them are given the title Benefactor. ²⁶ This must not happen with you. No; the greatest among you must behave as if he were the youngest, the leader as if he were the one who serves. ²⁷ For who is the greater: the one at the table or the one who serves? The one at table, surely? Yet here am I among you as one who serves!

²⁸ 'You are the men who have stood by me faithfully in my trials; ²⁹ and now I confer a kingdom on you, just as my Father conferred one on me: ³⁰ you will eat and drink at my table in my kingdom, and you will sit on thrones to judge the twelve tribes of Israel.

³¹ 'Simon, Simon! Satan, you must know, has got his wish to sift you all like wheat; ³² but I have prayed for you, Simon, that your faith may not fail, and once you have recovered, you in your turn must strengthen your brothers.' ³³ 'Lord,' he answered, 'I would be ready to go to prison with you, and to death.' ³⁴ Jesus replied, 'I tell you, Peter, by the time the cock crows today you will have denied three times that you know me.'

Jesus' words after supper set this meal and all our celebrations of the eucharist in a context of brotherly love. In taking the body and blood of Christ in communion, we involve ourselves in everyday life. At the end of the meal, Jesus announces Judas' treason. Judas has probably already taken communion. It is a terrifying warning: taking the body of Christ is no guarantee that we will not betray him! And the disciples choose this moment to squabble amongst themselves about who ranks highest! Whereas the eucharist ought above anything else to put us at the service of others ... This is what Jesus says to Peter. In spite of Peter's coming denial, Jesus chooses him from among his brothers to entrust with an important task; he will have to strengthen them in the faith.

Lord Jesus, we take your body and blood in communion, and too often we betray you by our cowardice, our mediocrity or our ambition.

We pray that, through your grace, our participation in the eucharist may strengthen our faith, assured in our hope and united as brothers in the service of all.

3. On the Mount of Olives, Jesus, the new Elijah, fights his supreme battle.

22 ³⁹ He then left to make his way as usual to the Mount of Olives, with the disciples following. ⁴⁰ When they reached the place he said to them, 'Pray not to be put to the test.'

⁴¹ Then he withdrew from them, about a stone's throw away, and knelt down and prayed. ⁴² 'Father,' he said, 'if you are willing, take this cup away from me. Nevertheless, let your will be done, not mine.' ⁴³ Then an angel appeared

to him, coming from heaven to give him strength. ⁴⁴ In his anguish he prayed even more earnestly, and his sweat fell to the ground like great drops of blood.

⁴⁵ When he rose from prayer he went to the disciples and found them sleeping for sheer grief. ⁴⁶ 'Why are you asleep?' he said to them. 'Get up and pray not to be put to the test.'

Jesus' agony is an incident in his passion. There, everything takes place in Christ's heart. This inner struggle is so fierce that Jesus' blood begins to flow as it will flow on the cross. All his humanity revolts against suffering and death, but at the same time he accepts the will of the one he tenderly calls 'Father'. On another occasion, an angel comforted the prophet Elijah when he was downcast; he gave him the strength to go on across the desert as far as Mount Horeb, where he had a mysterious vision of God. Jesus, the new Elijah, is also comforted by a messenger of God; he, too, goes deeply into the desert of his passion in order to reach the glory of God.

Lord Jesus, you emerged victorious from this agony, this tragic conflict. You gave yourself completely. At peace with yourself, you were able to be at the disposal of others throughout your passion.

Calm our fears and anxieties, soothe the sufferings of our sick brothers and sisters. Give us the strength to watch like you in prayer. Comfort all those who are weakened and weighed down.

4. Jesus is arrested.

22 ⁴⁷ He was still speaking when a number of men appeared, and at the head of them the man called Judas, one of the Twelve, who went up to Jesus to kiss him. ⁴⁸ Jesus said, 'Judas, are you betraying the Son of Man with a kiss?' ⁴⁹ His followers, seeing what was happening, said, 'Lord, shall we use our swords?' ⁵⁰ And one of them struck out at the high priest's servant, and cut off his right ear. ⁵¹ But at this Jesus spoke. 'Leave off!' he said 'That will do!' And touching the man's ear he healed him.

⁵² Then Jesus spoke to the chief priests and captains of the Temple guard and elders who had come for him. 'Am I a

brigand,' he said, 'that you had to set out with swords and clubs? ⁵³ When I was among you in the Temple day after day you never moved to lay hands on me. But this is your hour; this is the reign of darkness.'

With what calm and gentleness Jesus confronts his betrayer and those who come to lay hands on him. He shows his goodness by healing the high priest's servant who was wounded by one of his disciples. Jesus allows his enemies to arrest him, but he knows that they are only the pawns of the powers of darkness which he has come to subdue.

Lord Jesus, through your strength of spirit and your goodness, you are the victor over evil.

Teach us never to lose hope when we feel ourselves to be the pawns of forces which are too strong for us. Fill our hearts with loving kindness, even towards those who do not understand us, who persecute us or who despise us. Remember all those who are imprisoned or brought before courts; may they be treated with justice and mercy.

5. Peter, who denied Jesus, is transformed by a look from him.

22 ⁵⁴ They seized him then and led him away, and they took him to the high priest's house. Peter followed at a distance. ⁵⁵ They had lit a fire in the middle of the courtyard and Peter sat down among them, ⁵⁶ and as he was sitting there by the blaze a servant-girl saw him, peered at him, and said, 'This person was with him too.' ⁵⁷ But he denied it. 'Woman,' he said, 'I do not know him.' ⁵⁸ Shortly afterwards someone else saw him and said, 'You are another of them.' But Peter replied, 'I am not, my friend.' ⁵⁹ About an hour later another man insisted, saying, 'This fellow was certainly with him. Why, he is a Galilean.' ⁶⁰ 'My friend,' said Peter, 'I do not know what you are talking about.' At that instant, while he was still speaking, the cock crew, ⁶¹ and the Lord turned and looked straight at Peter, and Peter remembered what the Lord had said to him. 'Before

the cock crows today, you will have disowned me three times.' ⁶² And he went outside and wept bitterly.

⁶³ Meanwhile the men who guarded Jesus were mocking and beating him. ⁶⁴ They blindfolded him and questioned him. 'Play the prophet,' they said. 'Who hit you then?' ⁶⁵ And they continued heaping insults on him.

What appeal and what friendship there was in the look which Jesus turned upon Peter! This look reminds us that we are not truly penitent when we merely think about our sin, but only when we turn towards Christ our Saviour. It is no use being weighed down by remorse and guilt. We must turn our hearts towards the light of God. It is because we are sinners that Christ came. The awareness of our sin ought to throw us into God's arms with boundless confidence.

Lord Jesus, you heard Peter's denials, and you immediately and silently forgave him.
Forgive us our denials, our forgetfulness, our indifferences. Fortify our trust in your mercy. Give us the strength to pick ourselves up again when we fall and the courage to set off once more, with you for our support.

6. Before the Sanhedrin, Jesus declares himself to be the Messiah and the Son of God.

22 ⁶⁶ When day broke there was a meeting of the elders of the people, attended by the chief priests and scribes. He was brought before their council, ⁶⁷ and they said to him, 'If you are the Christ, tell us.' 'If I tell you,' he replied, 'you will not believe me, ⁶⁸ and if I question you, you will not answer. ⁶⁹ But from now on, the Son of Man will be seated at the right hand of the Power of God.' ⁷⁰ Then they all said, 'So you are the Son of God then?' He answered, 'It is you who say I am.' ⁷¹ 'What need of witnesses have we now?' they said. 'We have heard it for ourselves from his own lips.'

When the chief priests ask him if he is the Christ, the Messiah whom all men await, Jesus replies by alluding to the words of the prophet Daniel and of the psalms: Yes, he is the Son of Man, from now on enthroned over the whole world; yes, he will be seated at the right hand of God, that is to say, he will be part of the sovereignty and almighty power of God. To those who hear him it is blasphemy, and their second terrified and yet ironic question is charged with deep meaning: 'So you think you're the Son of God, then!' Jesus, with the utmost calm, fully accepts his responsibility: 'I am.' But by doing so he signs his death warrant.

Lord Jesus, you faced your judges as the Saviour Messiah and the Son of God. You told the truth without faltering, even though it cost you your life to do so.

Help us to be steadfast in our belief that you can redeem us because you are the Son of God. Give us a passion for the truth and the courage to be your witnesses whatever happens. May your reign of salvation and peace spread throughout the world.

*7. Pilate recognizes Jesus to be innocent and sends him to Herod.

23 ¹ The whole assembly then rose, and they brought him before Pilate.

² They began their accusation by saying, 'We found this man inciting our people to revolt, opposing payment of the tribute to Caesar, and claiming to be Christ, a king.' ³ Pilate put to him this question, 'Are you the king of the Jews?' 'It is you who say it,' he replied. ⁴ Pilate then said to the chief priests and the crowd, 'I find no case against this man.' ⁵ But they persisted. 'He is inflaming the people with his teaching all over Judaea; it has come all the way from Galilee, where he started, down to here.' ⁶ When Pilate heard this, he asked if the man were a Galilean; ⁷ and finding that he came under Herod's jurisdiction he passed him over to Herod who was also in Jerusalem at that time.

⁸ Herod was delighted to see Jesus; he had heard about him and had been wanting for a long time to set eyes on him; moreover, he was hoping to see some miracle worked by him. ⁹ So he questioned him at some length; but without getting any reply. ¹⁰ Meanwhile the chief priests and the

scribes were there, violently pressing their accusations.
¹¹ Then Herod, together with his guards, treated him with contempt and made fun of him; he put a rich cloak on him and sent him back to Pilate. ¹² And though Herod and Pilate had been enemies before, they were reconciled that same day.

To get him condemned by Pilate, the Jewish leaders treat Jesus' spiritual royalty – his messianic mission – as a political aspiration. However, Pilate has recognized Jesus' innocence, and he is to declare it twice more. Luke's narrative demonstrates quite clearly that Jesus dies through no fault of his own; he is truly the innocent victim and even Gentiles like Pilate were able to confirm this! As for Herod, he typifies superficial curiosity, unable to show a deep or open-minded interest in anything at all. Jesus remains silent before him, not in scorn, certainly, but more likely in deep pity.

Lord Jesus, you kept silent when you were made fun of.

Teach us to remain humble when we are misunderstood. But above all show us how always to respect the dignity of our fellow men, and give us the courage to stand up for those who are despised because of their poverty or their race.

8. Pilate delivers Jesus up to the whim of his enemies.

23 ¹³ Pilate then summoned the chief priests and the leading men and the people. ¹⁴ 'You brought this man before me,' he said, 'as a political agitator. Now I have gone into the matter myself in your presence and found no case against the man in respect of all the charges you bring against him. ¹⁵ Nor has Herod either, since he has sent him back to us. As you can see, the man has done nothing that deserves death, ¹⁶ so I shall have him flogged and then let him go.' ¹⁸ But as one man they howled, 'Away with him! Give us Barabbas!' ¹⁹ (This man had been thrown into prison for causing a riot in the city and for murder.)

²⁰ Pilate was anxious to set Jesus free and addressed them again ²¹ but they shouted back, 'Crucify him! Crucify him!'

²² And for the third time he spoke to them, 'Why? What harm has this man done? I have found no case against him that deserves death, so I shall have him punished and then let him go.' ²³ But they kept on shouting at the top of their voices, demanding that he should be crucified. And their shouts were growing louder.

²⁴ Pilate then gave his verdict: their demand was to be granted. ²⁵ He released the man they asked for, who had been imprisoned for rioting and murder, and handed Jesus over to them to deal with as they pleased.

For the third time, Pilate attests Jesus' innocence. What a lesson for Christians! If they are persecuted, let it be for their good behaviour and not for any fault in them. But Pilate gives way to the high priests; he releases the guilty one and delivers up the innocent.

With delicacy, St Luke passes in silence over the episode of the whipping as it is told by the other evangelists. He could not show his Lord humiliated in this way. Perhaps he also wanted to make us understand that the greatest drama of the passion took place in Jesus' soul. It was in Gethsemane that Jesus first of all poured out his blood.

Lord Jesus, your life was exchanged for the life of a murderer; you died for all us sinners.

Forgive us our sins. Forgive the sins of all men throughout the world. May your mercy lead all mankind towards true justice, real love and peace – not the peace which is merely a truce, but peace which reigns in our hearts.

*9. Simon from Cyrene and the women take part in Jesus' passion.

23 ²⁶ As they were leading him away they seized on a man, Simon from Cyrene, who was coming in from the country, and made him shoulder the cross and carry it behind Jesus. ²⁷ Large numbers of people followed him, and of women too, who mourned and lamented for him. ²⁸ But Jesus turned to them and said, 'Daughters of Jerusalem, do not weep for

me; weep rather for yourselves and for your children. ²⁹ For the days will surely come when people will say, "Happy are those who are barren, the wombs that have never borne, the breasts that have never suckled!" ³⁰ Then they will begin to say to the mountains, "Fall on us!"; to the hills, "Cover us!" ³¹ For if men use the green wood like this, what will happen when it is dry?' ³² Now with him they were also leading out two other criminals to be executed.

Simon is made to carry the cross behind Jesus. In this way he becomes the pattern of a disciple walking behind his master. For Jesus has given us clear warning that whoever would follow him as his disciple must carry his cross.

Because, in Gethsemane, Jesus has won a victory over suffering by facing up to it calmly and accepting it as the Father's will, he is now at peace and able to forget his own suffering to concern himself with that of others. Several women, some of those who have been with him while he travelled about preaching, are following him, weeping. He tries to prepare them – them and the people whom they symbolize – for the tragedy which awaits them: the fall of Jerusalem and the suffering of the Jewish people.

Lord Jesus, you are led out to execution with criminals; you are the Suffering Servant put on a level with wicked men; you see in your own destiny the tragedy of your people and of all those who are persecuted for their faith and in the name of justice.

Have mercy on us. Have mercy on sinners. Have mercy on the world. Save us.

*10. Jesus is crucified. His first words are of forgiveness.

23 ³³ When they reached the place called The Skull, they crucified him there and the two criminals also, one on the right, the other on the left. ³⁴ Jesus said, 'Father, forgive them; they do not know what they are doing.' Then they cast lots to share out his clothing.

³⁵ The people stayed there watching him. As for the leaders, they jeered at him. 'He saved others,' they said, 'let him save himself if he is the Christ of God, the Chosen One.'

36 The soldiers mocked him too, and when they approached to offer him vinegar **37** they said, 'If you are the king of the Jews, save yourself.' **38** Above him there was an inscription: 'This is the King of the Jews.'

Jesus triumphs over evil by standing his ground, that is to say in biblical terms by his way of 'holding up' when being tested because he knows that he is being upheld by God. He is able to overcome evil by forgiveness. Only someone who is tortured can forgive his torturers. And this forgiveness, this gift above all other gifts, is the climax of his love and the most outstanding feature of his life according to the Gospel. Jesus himself cannot be at peace with the Father unless all men, and most of all those who torture him, are at peace with him as well.

The people are silent and respectful. The religious leaders taunt Jesus with the title 'Messiah' which he had claimed, and the soldiers mock him with the title of 'king'.

Lord Jesus, you prayed for your torturers. Pour such love into our hearts that we are always able to forgive. The world is steeped in the blood of so much hatred and revenge; may all Christians set an example of mercy.

*11. The next words of the crucified Jesus open the gates of Paradise to a criminal.

23 **39** One of the criminals hanging there abused him. 'Are you not the Christ?' he said. 'Save yourself and us as well.' **40** But the other spoke up and rebuked him. 'Have you no fear of God at all?' he said. 'You got the same sentence as he did, **41** but in our case we deserved it: we are paying for what we did. But this man has done nothing wrong. **42** Jesus,' he said, 'remember me when you come into your kingdom.' **43** 'Indeed, I promise you,' he replied, 'today you will be with me in paradise.'

A conversion takes place on the cross. St Luke paints a moving picture of the faith shown by the criminal crucified with Jesus. This man speaks to him with wonderful confidence, and calls him simply by his name, 'Jesus', as did the ten lepers on another occasion. He speaks to him as he would to God, repeating a

Jewish prayer spoken by the dying: 'Remember me'. And he affirms the kingship of this man who is being crucified. Jesus responds to this remarkable faith with quiet certainty; today is the day of salvation which he has so often proclaimed.

Lord Jesus, you forgot your own suffering to make the penitent thief welcome.
Remember us sinners at the hour of our death. Receive us into your kingdom with you. And let your mercy reach out to all our fellow men throughout the world.

*12. Jesus speaks to his Father from the cross.

23 ⁴⁴ It was now about the sixth hour and, with the sun eclipsed, a darkness came over the whole land until the ninth hour. ⁴⁵ The veil of the Temple was torn right down the middle; ⁴⁶ and when Jesus had cried out in a loud voice, he said, 'Father, into your hands I commit my spirit.' With these words he breathed his last.

⁴⁷ When the centurion saw what had taken place, he gave praise to God and said, 'This was a great and good man.' ⁴⁸ And when all the people who had gathered for the spectacle saw what had happened, they went home beating their breasts.

⁴⁹ All his friends stood at a distance; so also did the women who had accompanied him from Galilee, and they saw all this happen.

In Luke's Gospel, the first words Jesus speaks are about his Father: 'Do you not know that I must be busy with my Father's affairs?' he says to his parents. The last words of his human life are to abandon himself to the Father. Jesus had reached the depths of despair in Gethsemane, and had emerged victorious. At peace, he was able to end his life as a Jew ends his day, by repeating this psalm of trust: 'Into your hands I commit my spirit.'

Jesus' death makes conversion possible: the conversion of the Gentile officer who recognizes Jesus' innocence and gives praise to God, and the conversion of the bystanders, who beat their breasts; and it is a call to his closest friends, who remain there contemplating so great a mystery.

Lord Jesus, you died for us.
We believe in you, we worship you, we gave thanks to the Father for your passion, for your cross and for your sacred death. May you be every day more and more the Saviour of the world.

13. The peace of the tomb.

> 23 ⁵⁰ Then a member of the council arrived, an upright and virtuous man named Joseph. ⁵¹ He had not consented to what the others had planned and carried out. He came from Arimathaea, a Jewish town, and he lived in the hope of seeing the kingdom of God. ⁵² This man went to Pilate and asked for the body of Jesus. ⁵³ He then took it down, wrapped it in a shroud and put him in a tomb which was hewn in stone in which no one had yet been laid. ⁵⁴ It was Preparation Day and the sabbath was imminent.
> ⁵⁵ Meanwhile the women who had come from Galilee with Jesus were following behind. They took note of the tomb and of the position of the body.
> ⁵⁶ Then they returned and prepared spices and ointments. And on the sabbath day they rested, as the Law required.

The narrative reaches a time of peace and waiting. There is nothing left to feel but the gentleness of Jesus' friends – Joseph of Arimathaea, a good, just and upright man, and the women who are making themselves ready to pay Jesus their last respects.

They are all waiting for something, but they do not yet know that what will happen will exceed all their expectations. The narrative does in fact hint at it. The tomb is a new one, and the lamps of the sabbath begin to shine out, harbingers of a different kind of light. The sabbath, the seventh day of creation on which God rested from his labours, is about to give way to the eighth, the day when eternal life begins.

Lord Jesus, you have experienced death.
We entrust to you all those we have known who have died. Grant them

peace. And keep us in the hope of the resurrection and of eternal life in the kingdom of God.

*14. The tomb is open! The Lord Jesus is alive!

24 ¹ On the first day of the week, at the first sign of dawn, they went to the tomb with the spices they had prepared. ² They found that the stone had been rolled away from the tomb, ³ but on entering discovered that the body of the Lord Jesus was not there. ⁴ As they stood there not knowing what to think, two men in brilliant clothes suddenly appeared at their side. ⁵ Terrified, the women lowered their eyes. But the two men said to them, 'Why look among the dead for someone who is alive? ⁶ He is not here; he has risen. Remember what he told you when he was still in Galilee: ⁷ that the Son of Man had to be handed over into the power of sinful men and be crucified, and rise again on the third day.' ⁸ And they remembered his words.

⁹ When the women returned from the tomb they told all this to the Eleven and to all the others. ¹⁰ The women were Mary of Magdala, Joanna, and Mary the mother of James. The other women with them also told the apostles, ¹¹ but this story of theirs seemed pure nonsense, and they did not believe them.

¹² Peter, however, went running to the tomb. He bent down and saw the binding cloths but nothing else; he then went back home, amazed at what had happened.

The women come to anoint a corpse; they are given a message. They come to embalm the dead Jesus; God tells them that the Lord Jesus is alive!

For St Luke, Galilee does not lie in the future, at the end of the road; it belongs to the past as the place where Jesus told his disciples what would happen. The whole mystery of Jesus reaches its climax and fulfilment in Jerusalem. It is only in the book of Acts that the message will travel to the end of the earth.

The women believe because of what Jesus has told them. Peter sees for himself and does not believe. The Risen Lord has to explain to him what was written in the scriptures.

Lord Jesus, the women were the first to believe in you on Easter Day and no one would listen to them. You once gave thanks to the Father because such things were concealed from wise and learned men and revealed to infants.

May our hearts become as innocent as children's so that we may receive the Good News. And may your Holy Spirit guide us to understand your word and make us grow in faith day by day.

Conclusion: Two disciples meet with Jesus on the road to Emmaus.

24 ¹³ That very same day, two of them were on their way to a village called Emmaus, seven miles from Jerusalem, ¹⁴ and they were talking together about all that had happened. ¹⁵ Now as they talked this over, Jesus himself came up and walked by their side; ¹⁶ but something prevented them from recognizing him. ¹⁷ He said to them, 'What matters are you discussing as you walk along?' They stopped short, their faces downcast.

¹⁸ Then one of them, called Cleopas, answered him: 'You must be the only person staying in Jerusalem who does not know the things that have been happening there these last few days.' ¹⁹ 'What things?' he asked. 'All about Jesus of Nazareth,' they answered, 'who proved he was a great prophet by the things he said and did in the sight of God and of the whole people; ²⁰ and how our chief priests and our leaders handed him over to be sentenced to death, and had him crucified. ²¹ Our own hope had been that he would be the one to set Israel free. And this is not all: two whole days have gone by since it all happened; ²² and some women from our group have astounded us: they went to the tomb in the early morning, ²³ and when they did not find the body, they came back to tell us they had seen a vision of angels who declared he was alive. ²⁴ Some of our friends went to the tomb and found everything exactly as the women had reported, but of him they saw nothing.'

²⁵ Then he said to them, 'You foolish men! So slow to believe the full message of the prophets! ²⁶ Was it not ordained that the Christ should suffer and so enter into his

glory?' ²⁷ Then, starting with Moses and going through all the prophets, he explained to them the passages throughout the scriptures that were about himself.

²⁸ When they drew near to the village to which they were going, he made as if to go on; ²⁹ but they pressed him to stay with them. 'It is nearly evening,' they said, 'and the day is almost over.' So he went in to stay with them. ³⁰ Now while he was with them at table, he took the bread and said the blessing; then he broke it and handed it to them. ³¹ And their eyes were opened and they recognized him; but he had vanished from their sight. ³² Then they said to each other, 'Did not our hearts burn within us as he talked to us on the road and explained the scriptures to us?'

³³ They set out that instant and returned to Jerusalem. There they found the Eleven assembled together with their companions, ³⁴ who said to them, 'Yes, it is true. The Lord has risen and has appeared to Simon.' ³⁵ Then they told their story of what had happened on the road and how they had recognized him at the breaking of bread.

In St Luke's Gospel, the whole of Jesus' life has been an 'ascent' to Jerusalem. But the two disciples are going away from Jerusalem! Luke could not indicate more clearly that they are abandoning Jesus' way. Yet they are thinking about him and discussing him, even to the point of telling their unknown companion about his life, with which they are perfectly familiar . . . But none of that has any meaning for them any more. So it is possible to know Jesus and be able to discuss him, and yet not recognize him! Then what has he to do to make us?

The Risen Christ has to explain the scriptures to us himself. Then the meaning of his life becomes clear. Then, with our hearts aflame, we can recognize him walking beside us and offering himself to us in the eucharist. Something prevented the disciples from recognizing him; now their eyes are open because Jesus has explained the scriptures to them. They do not recognize him; but the Risen Christ makes himself known to them. At the open tomb, Peter did not see Jesus; but the Lord appeared to Peter!

And so it is not for the disciples to see and recognize Jesus; it is the Risen Christ who makes himself visible and makes himself recognized. He has been there throughout history, continuing to explain the scriptures.

Lord Jesus, we have meditated on your passion and death and we rejoice in your resurrection.

Keep us in faith, and peace and love. Inspire in us a love of the scriptures, the revelation of your Word. And may the Good News lead us to greater love and service of our fellow men.

The Road to the Cross according to

St John

Introduction: **On his entry into Jerusalem on Palm Sunday, Jesus announces his death and his glory.**

12 ²⁰ Among those who went up to worship at the festival were some Greeks. ²¹ These approached Philip, who came from Bethsaida in Galilee, and put this request to him. 'Sir, we should like to see Jesus.' ²² Philip went to tell Andrew, and Andrew and Philip together went to tell Jesus.

²³ Jesus replied to them:

'Now the hour has come
for the Son of Man to be glorified.
²⁴ I tell you, most solemnly,
unless a wheat grain falls on the ground and dies,
it remains only a single grain;
but if it dies,
it yields a rich harvest.
²⁵ Anyone who loves his life loses it;
anyone who hates his life in this world
will keep it for the eternal life.
²⁶ If a man serves me, he must follow me,
wherever I am, my servant will be there too.
If anyone serves me, my Father will honour him.
²⁷ Now my soul is troubled.
What shall I say:
Father, save me from this hour?
But it was for this very reason that I have come to this hour.
²⁸ Father, glorify your name!'

A voice came from heaven, 'I have glorified it, and I will glorify it again.'

²⁹ People standing by, who heard this, said it was a clap of thunder; others said, 'It was an angel speaking to him.' ³⁰ Jesus answered, 'It was not for my sake that this voice came, but for yours.

> ³¹ 'Now sentence is being passed on this world;
> now the price of this world is to be overthrown.
> ³² And when I am lifted up from the earth,
> I shall draw all men to myself.'

³³ By these words he indicated the kind of death he would die.

Jesus knows that he is to die. The hour has come for him to be glorified. For him, death is only the beginning of his victory over the forces of evil. He will be lifted up; lifted up on the cross like a guilty slave; lifted up to the Father as his glorious Son. He is certain of this, and yet his soul is troubled. 'Father, save me,' he says. God's answer is a mysterious one. He cannot fail him. Will the disciples be able to follow him and die like a grain of wheat to bring forth fruit in love?

Lord Jesus, you welcomed Greeks equally with Jews, and you invited everyone to serve you and follow you into your Father's kingdom.

May we, like you, die to ourselves in service to our fellow men, wherever they are. Keep us steadfast, so that even when put to the test we do not lose hope of sharing in your life and your glory.

*1. Jesus washes his disciples' feet.

13 ¹ It was before the festival of the Passover, and Jesus knew that the hour had come for him to pass from this world to the Father. He had always loved those who were his in the world, but now he showed how perfect his love was.

² They were at supper, and the devil had already put it into the mind of Judas Iscariot son of Simon, to betray him. ³ Jesus knew that the Father had put everything into his hands, and that he had come from God and was returning to God, ⁴ and he got up from table, removed his outer gar-

ment and, taking a towel, wrapped it round his waist; ⁵ he then poured water into a basin and began to wash the disciples' feet and to wipe them with the towel he was wearing.

⁶ He came to Simon Peter, who said to him, 'Lord, are you going to wash my feet?' ⁷ Jesus answered, 'At the moment you do not know what I am doing, but later you will understand.' ⁸ 'Never!' said Peter. 'You shall never wash my feet.' Jesus replied, 'If I do not wash you, you can have nothing in common with me.' ⁹ 'Then, Lord,' said Simon Peter, 'not only my feet, but my hands and my head as well!' ¹⁰ Jesus said, 'No one who has taken a bath needs washing, he is clean all over. You too are clean, though not all of you are.' ¹¹ He knew who was going to betray him; that was why he said, 'though not all of you are.'

¹² When he had washed their feet and put on his clothes again he went back to the table. 'Do you understand,' he said, 'what I have done to you? ¹³ You call me Master and Lord, and rightly; so I am. ¹⁴ If I, then, the Lord and Master, have washed your feet, you should wash each other's feet. ¹⁵ I have given you an example so that you may copy what I have done to you.

¹⁶ 'I tell you most solemnly,
   no servant is greater than his master,
   no messenger is greater than the man who sent him.

¹⁷ 'Now that you know this, happiness will be yours if you behave accordingly.'

To wash travellers' feet was a gesture of friendship and respect towards those for whom it was done. The women who performed the action for Jesus realized this. But the task was usually delegated to the lowest of the servants, and most often to the slaves. So Jesus knowingly performs the task of a slave for his disciples, and this is what upsets Simon Peter so deeply. He does not see that his master's action is a summing up of all that he had come to do: to serve and to cleanse.

Lord Jesus, to be God's perfect servant you made yourself the servant of your brother men, and you did so again when, nailed to the cross, you cleansed the world with your blood.

Teach us to serve you humbly by putting ourselves every day at the service of our fellow men, and giving without counting the cost.

*2. Before enduring his passion, Jesus prays for his disciples.

17 ¹ After saying this, Jesus raised his eyes to heaven and said:

'Father, the hour has come:
glorify your Son
so that your Son may glorify you;
² and, through the power over all mankind that you have given him,
let him give eternal life to all those you have entrusted to him.
³ And eternal life is this:
to know you,
the only true God,
and Jesus Christ whom you have sent.
⁴ I have glorified you on earth
and finished the work
that you gave me to do.
⁵ Now, Father, it is time for you to glorify me
with that glory I had with you
before ever the world was.
I have made your name known
⁶ to the men you took from the world to give me.
They were yours and you gave them to me,
and they have kept your word.
. . . .
¹⁸ As you sent me into the world,
I have sent them into the world,
¹⁹ and for their sake I consecrate myself
so that they too may be consecrated in truth.
²⁰ I pray not only for these,
but for those also
who through their words will believe in me.

ACCORDING TO ST JOHN

²¹ May they all be one.
Father, may they be one in us,
as you are in me and I am in you,
so that the world may believe it was you who sent me.
²² I have given them the glory you gave to me,
that they may be one as we are one.
²³ With me in them and you in me,
may they be so completely one
that the world will realize that it was you who sent me
and that I have loved them as much as you loved me.'

After talking at length with his disciples and before leaving the room where the last supper has been held, Jesus speaks to his Father. We usually call this fine prayer 'the High Priestly prayer'. It is one in which Jesus offers himself to his Father, and pleads for those who believe in his word. On the eve of his own sacrifice, the Christ appears in this way as the one true priest, the one true Saviour. His disciples and their successors throughout the ages will carry on his mission, and Jesus asks the Father to keep them in holiness, truth and unity, so that the world will believe their words as if they were his own.

Lord Jesus, you offered your life to the Father to keep your disciples in unity.

Deepen our faith so that we may come to understand you as the one true God; teach us to embrace the truth of your word. And as we gaze at the cross, may we set aside everything that divides and separates us from our brothers and sisters.

3. Jesus allows himself to be arrested.

18 ¹ After he had said all this Jesus left with his disciples and crossed the Kedron valley. There was a garden there, and he went into it with his disciples. ² Judas the traitor knew the place well, since Jesus had often met his disciples there, ³ and he brought the cohort to this place together with a detachment of guards sent by the chief priests and the Pharisees, all with lanterns and torches and weapons. ⁴ Knowing everything that was going to happen to him,

Jesus then came forward and said, 'Who are you looking for?' ⁵ They answered, 'Jesus the Nazarene.' He said, 'I am he.' Now Judas the traitor was standing among them. ⁶ When Jesus said, 'I am he,' they moved back and fell to the ground. ⁷ He asked them a second time, 'Who are you looking for?' They said, 'Jesus the Nazarene.' ⁸ 'I have told you that I am he,' replied Jesus. 'If I am the one you are looking for, let these others go.' ⁹ This was to fulfil the words he had spoken, 'Not one of those you gave me have I lost.'

¹⁰ Simon Peter, who carried a sword, drew it and wounded the high priest's servant, cutting off his right ear. The servant's name was Malchus. ¹¹ Jesus said to Peter, 'Put your sword back in its scabbard; am I not to drink the cup that the Father has given me?'

¹² The cohort and its captain and the Jewish guards seized Jesus and bound him.

John in his Gospel emphasizes that Jesus knows all that is going to happen to him. For him one thing is clear; even during his passion, Jesus is still the Master, Christ the king, and nothing takes place that he does not freely accept. And so Jesus, far from trying to escape, goes towards the soldiers and speaks to them first: 'Who are you looking for?' Immediately, he indicates himself: 'I am he,' with a play on words which recalls the name of God himself: 'I am.' On another occasion he had dared to say: 'Before Abraham was, I am.' He is indeed the serene Son of God who asks freedom for his disciples and encourages them not to use violence at this dreadful moment.

Lord Jesus, you did not refuse the cup which the Father gave you to drink, and in allowing yourself to be handed over to your enemies, you gained salvation for your disciples.

Show us how to obey the Father's will day by day. And teach us to forget our own problems in concern for others.

4. Jesus appears before the Jewish high priest.

18 ¹³ They took him first to Annas, because Annas was the father-in-law of Caiaphas, who was high priest that year.

¹⁴ It was Caiaphas who had suggested to the Jews, 'It is better for one man to die for the people.'
. . . .

¹⁹ The high priest questioned Jesus about his disciples and his teaching. ²⁰ Jesus answered, 'I have spoken openly for all the world to hear; I have always taught in the synagogue and in the Temple where all the Jews meet together: I have said nothing in secret. ²¹ But why ask me? Ask my hearers what I taught: they know what I said.' ²² At these words, one of the guards standing by gave Jesus a slap in the face, saying, 'Is that the way to answer the high priest?' ²³ Jesus replied, 'If there is something wrong in what I said, point it out; but if there is no offence in it, why do you strike me?' ²⁴ Then Annas sent him, still bound, to Caiaphas the high priest.

Jesus gives a simple reply to the high priest, but he in his turn asks a question. Instead of being interrogated, he becomes the interrogator; from being the accused, he turns into the judge. Everyone understands what is happening, even the guards, and one of them strikes him for his insolence. But Jesus stays calm, master of the situation. No one dares answer him, nor ask him any more questions. He never seems greater to us than when he is most humiliated.

Lord Jesus, you were struck by a soldier. We pray to you for all those throughout the world who are unjustly arrested and persecuted. We pray for those who are tortured and imprisoned. We pray too for their torturers and gaolers.

Grant freedom to those who have none. Raise up those who have been stripped of dignity. Forgive us our injustices, our pride, our cruelty. May your reign of justice and love come to the world.

5. Jesus is led before Pilate.

18 ²⁸ They then led Jesus from the house of Caiaphas to the Praetorium. It was now morning. They did not go into the Praetorium themselves or they would be defiled and unable to eat the passover. ²⁹ So Pilate came outside to them and

said, 'What charge do you bring against this man?' They replied, ³⁰ 'If he were not a criminal, we should not be handing him over to you.' ³¹ Pilate said, 'Take him yourselves, and try him by your own Law.' The Jews answered, 'We are not allowed to put a man to death.' ³² This was to fulfil the words Jesus had spoken indicating the way he was going to die.

³³ So Pilate went back into the Praetorium and called Jesus to him. 'Are you the king of the Jews?' he asked. ³⁴ Jesus replied, 'Do you ask this of your own accord, or have others spoken to you about me?' ³⁵ Pilate answered, 'Am I a Jew? It is your own people and the chief priests who have handed you over to me: what have you done?' ³⁶ Jesus replied, 'Mine is not a kingdom of this world; if my kingdom were of this world, my men would have fought to prevent my being surrendered to the Jews. But my kingdom is not of this kind.' ³⁷ 'So you are a king then?' said Pilate. 'It is you who say it,' answered Jesus. 'Yes, I am a king. I was born for this, I came into the world for this: to bear witness to the truth; and all who are on the side of truth listen to my voice.' ³⁸ 'Truth?' said Pilate. 'What is that?'; and with that he went out again to the Jews and said, 'I find no case against him. ³⁹ But according to a custom of yours I should release one prisoner at the Passover; would you like me, then, to release the king of the Jews?' ⁴⁰ At this they shouted: 'Not this man,' they said, 'but Barabbas.' Barabbas was a brigand.

We can well imagine the contemptuous irony with which Pilate says to Jesus: 'Are you the king of the Jews?' But Jesus stays quite calm and, as with the high priest, he reverses their roles. The one being interrogated becomes the interrogator: 'Do you ask this of your own accord?' Pilate answers impatiently, sharply. Jesus quietly talks to him about his kingship, which cannot be defended by weapons because it is completely bound up with his mission to make known the truth about God and man. But Pilate is far too preoccupied with his personal ambitions to attach any importance to his prisoner's words.

Lord Jesus, your life was exchanged for that of Barabbas. You came for thieves and sinners and lost sheep.

May your Holy Spirit shine upon us so that we can recognize our sin, and acknowledge you as our Saviour and our king.

6. The soldiers hail Jesus as 'king'.

19 ¹ Pilate then had Jesus taken away and scourged; ² and after this, the soldiers twisted some thorns into a crown and put it on his head, and dressed him in a purple robe. ³ They kept coming up to him and saying, 'Hail, king of the Jews!'; and they slapped him in the face.

⁴ Pilate came outside again and said to them, 'Look, I am going to bring him out to you to let you see that I find no case.' ⁵ Jesus then came out wearing the crown of thorns and the purple robe. Pilate said, 'Here is the man.'

Jesus is handed over to the soldiers, who call him 'king' in mockery. The crown of thorns and the purple robe are the emblems of his wretched kingship. But all the time Christ truly is king. His kingship is indeed very different from those of this world, but it is real in the eyes of God and of all those who are ready to believe in the scandal of the cross.

Lord Jesus, they scoffed at you and mocked you, and brought you out crying, 'Here is the man!' Yes, you are every man who is persecuted, every man who suffers, every man who grieves. Here is the man who is going to die, as every one will die. Here is the man who will rise again and enfold mankind – redeemed, ennobled, saved – in his new life.

May your passion bring salvation to all our fellow men who are in trouble, or under tyranny, or bowed down by sin. Give us the eyes to see that every one, even the humblest and poorest, has the royal dignity of being a Son of God. Teach us to fight without ceasing to safeguard that dignity.

*7. Jesus is proclaimed 'king' by Pilate.

19 ⁶ When they saw him the chief priests and the guards shouted, 'Crucify him! Crucify him!' Pilate said, 'Take him yourselves and crucify him: I can find no case against him.'

⁷ 'We have a Law,' the Jews replied, 'and according to that Law he ought to die, because he has claimed to be the Son of God.'

⁸ When Pilate heard them say this his fears increased. ⁹ Re-entering the Praetorium, he said to Jesus, 'Where do you come from?' But Jesus made no answer. ¹⁰ Pilate then said to him, 'Are you refusing to speak to me? Surely you know I have power to release you and I have power to crucify you?' ¹¹ 'You would have no power over me,' replied Jesus, 'if it had not been given you from above; that is why the one who handed me over to you has the greater guilt.'

¹² From that moment Pilate was anxious to set him free, but the Jews shouted, 'If you set him free you are no friend of Caesar's; anyone who makes himself king is defying Caesar.' ¹³ Hearing these words, Pilate had Jesus brought out, and seated himself on the chair of judgment at a place called the Pavement, in Hebrew Gabbatha. ¹⁴ It was Passover Preparation Day, about the sixth hour. 'Here is your king,' said Pilate to the Jews. ¹⁵ 'Take him away, take him away!' they said. 'Crucify him!' 'Do you want me to crucify your king?' said Pilate. The chief priests answered, 'We have no king except Caesar.' ¹⁶ So in the end Pilate handed him over to them to be crucified.

At the very moment when he is about to be handed over to his executioners, Jesus seems to be forgotten, pushed into the background, as if he were not the one at stake in the argument between the chief priests and Pilate. The procurator is more anxious to humiliate the chief priests than to pass a fair judgment on the condemned man who is proving so troublesome. That is why he says with such scornful irony, when he brings Jesus out to them: 'Behold your king!' But the Jews take this opportunity to force the hated Roman to show his cowardice and fear of the Emperor. In retaliation, the governor manages to make the high priests shout that they have no king but Caesar, who is held in contempt by everyone. But Jesus says nothing.

Lord Jesus, you kept silent while the crowd was screaming at you, even though you were the subject of their sordid quarrelling.

Teach us to remain calm and at prayer, abandoning ourselves to God, even at the most difficult moments. Give strength to all those who have to be silent under persecution, and keep them in hope and faith.

8. The crucified king.

19 ¹⁶ They then took charge of Jesus, ¹⁷ and carrying his own cross he went out of the city to the place of the skull or, as it was called in Hebrew, Golgotha, ¹⁸ where they crucified him with two others, one on either side with Jesus in the middle. ¹⁹ Pilate wrote out a notice and had it fixed to the cross; it ran: 'Jesus the Nazarene, King of the Jews'. ²⁰ This notice was read by many of the Jews, because the place where Jesus was crucified was not far from the city, and the writing was in Hebrew, Latin and Greek. ²¹ So the Jewish chief priests said to Pilate, 'You should not write "King of the Jews", but "This man said: I am King of the Jews."' ²² Pilate answered, 'What I have written, I have written.'

²³ When the soldiers had finished crucifying Jesus they took his clothing and divided it into four shares, one for each soldier. His undergarment was seamless, woven in one piece from neck to hem; ²⁴ so they said to one another, 'Instead of tearing it, let's throw dice to decide who is to have it.' In this way the words of scripture were fulfilled:

They shared out my clothing among them.
They cast lots for my clothes.

This is exactly what the soldiers did.

To humiliate his enemies, the Jewish chiefs, as much as he possibly can Pilate has this notice put up: 'Jesus the Nazarene, King of the Jews'. It is written in the common language of the time; Hebrew, spoken in Palestine; Greek, used as an international language throughout the Mediterranean; and Latin, the official language of the Roman Empire. By affecting to crucify a king of the Jews, Pilate shows his hearty scorn for their race. This title of king which Jesus' accusers and judges constantly throw in his face makes a deep impression on John, who saw all these things and believed. For him, the wretched man scorned and nailed to the cross is, without a doubt, the king foretold by the prophets, and although Pilate did not intend it thus, his notice proclaims but the truth: Jesus is king, not only of the Jews, but of Greeks, of Romans, of the whole world.

Lord Jesus, crucified under the name of king, you have made us see that true royal power is found in love and the gift of self to the very end.

Show us how to share in your kingship by serving and loving you, by serving and loving our fellow men, especially those who are distressed or weighed down by care.

*9. Jesus and his mother.

> 19 ²⁵ Near the cross of Jesus stood his mother and his mother's sister, Mary the wife of Clopas, and Mary of Magdala. ²⁶ Seeing his mother and the disciple he loved standing near her, Jesus said to his mother, 'Woman, this is your son.' ²⁷ Then to the disciple he said, 'This is your mother.' And from that moment the disciple made a place for her in his home.

In the Bible, it is unusual for a son to call his mother 'woman'. But John had already recorded Jesus' use of the word to his mother before at the time of his first miracle at the wedding in Cana. Jesus said then, 'Woman, what do you want of me? My hour has not yet come!' Now the hour has come, the hour of his supreme gift, the hour of his real glory in the eyes of God, and the same word falls from the lips of the crucified Jesus. So Mary becomes the Woman *par excellence*, linked in humility with him of whom Pilate said, 'Here is the Man.' This final gesture of Jesus in entrusting Mary and John each to the other's care is more than a simple act of filial piety. Like a new Eve, but in complete contrast to the first one, Mary becomes the mother of all believers, who are represented by the beloved disciple.

Lord Jesus, as you were being crucified you entrusted your mother to your disciple and your disciple to your mother.

May we put our trust in her to lead us to you. And may she always be a model in your Church to the faithful and a constant sign of your tenderness.

*10. Jesus dies on the cross.

19 ²⁸ After this, Jesus knew that everything had now been completed, and to fulfil the scripture perfectly he said:

'I am thirsty.'

²⁹ A jar full of vinegar stood there, so putting a sponge soaked in the vinegar on a hyssop stick they held it up to his mouth. ²⁹ After Jesus had taken the vinegar he said, 'It is accomplished'; and bowing his head he gave up his spirit.

John records only three words of Jesus from the cross. One is for his mother. The second is, 'I am thirsty.' The Gospel often speaks of thirst and of living water, and it is quite probable that Jesus' cry is not only one of need from his tortured body, but also a cry from his soul to the Father for the salvation of the world. John has already prepared us for the third word, 'It is accomplished,' by writing 'Jesus knew that everything had now been completed . . .' and he relates this to help us understand and believe that at this moment Jesus knows he has completed the task his Father sent him to do.

Lord Jesus, dying on the cross, you can rest now, you have finished your task; you can commit your spirit freely to the Father, you can send your Holy Spirit on the apostles. The redemption of the world has been won!

We praise you, we bless you, we worship you, we glorify you, we give you thanks for your great glory. You alone are the Most High: Jesus Christ, with the Holy Spirit, in the glory of God the Father. Amen.

*11. A soldier pierces Jesus' side with a lance.

19 ³¹ It was Preparation Day, and to prevent the bodies remaining on the cross during the sabbath – since that sabbath was a day of special solemnity – the Jews asked Pilate to have the legs broken and the bodies taken away. ³² Consequently the soldiers came and broke the legs of the first

man who had been crucified with him and then of the other. ³³ When they came to Jesus, they found he was already dead, and so instead of breaking his legs ³⁴ one of the soldiers pierced his side with a lance; and immediately there came out blood and water. ³⁵ This is the evidence of one who saw it – trustworthy evidence, and he knows he speaks the truth – and he gives it so that you may believe as well. ³⁶ Because all this happened to fulfil the words of scripture:

Not one bone of his will be broken;

³⁷and again, in another place scripture says:

They will look on the one whom they have pierced.

The gravity with which John declares himself to be a witness of the action which caused blood and water to flow from Jesus' side shows that he attached a great deal of importance to it. To be correct, it was probably not water but colourless fluid. Whatever it was, the text which John quotes and which he applies to Jesus – 'Not one bone of his will be broken' – refers to the paschal lamb which the Jews used to sacrifice as a thank offering for their deliverance from slavery in Egypt. The true lamb who brings freedom is therefore Christ Jesus. The blood which flows from his side shows that his sacrifice is real. The water is the symbol of the Holy Spirit: 'From his breast shall flow fountains of living water.' Jesus had said that about the Spirit which those who believed in him were to receive. All these mysterious sayings were fulfilled on Calvary. In the eyes of his enemies Jesus was unquestionably conquered. In the eyes of the faithful, even before he rose living from the tomb, he was unquestionably the conqueror.

Lord Jesus, you have washed us with the Holy Spirit in the waters of baptism. You feed us with your body and you bathe us in your blood when they are offered in the eucharist.

May we look on your pierced heart, and humbly accept the evidence of your beloved disciple so that we may believe as well.

12. Jesus is laid in the tomb

19 ³⁸ After this, Joseph of Arimathaea, who was a disciple of Jesus – though a secret one because he was afraid of the Jews – asked Pilate to let him remove the body of Jesus. Pilate gave permission, so they came and took it away. ³⁹ Nicodemus came as well – the same one who had first come to Jesus at night-time – and he brought a mixture of myrrh and aloes, weighing about a hundred pounds. ⁴⁰ They took the body of Jesus and wrapped it with the spices in linen cloths, following the Jewish burial custom. ⁴¹ At the place where he had been crucified there was a garden, and in this garden a new tomb in which no one had yet been buried. ⁴² Since it was the Jewish Day of Preparation and the tomb was near at hand, they laid Jesus there.

Since the solemn sabbath day of the Passover would begin at nightfall, Jesus was buried hastily; it was not permitted to bury the dead on the sabbath day, any more than it was to do work of any kind or travel any distance. So the tomb would be undisturbed during the whole of the Saturday. The disciples were still very loyal to the Jewish observances. Perhaps they were also fearful of arousing the anger of the Pharisees if they were caught defying the Law. So it was not until Sunday morning that some of the women came back. But the Sunday morning was to bring in the new Passover.

Lord Jesus, you loved us so much that you gave your life for us. You could say, 'I am the resurrection and the life,' and yet you accepted death.

Help us to accept our death. May we make this acceptance an act of love and faith by living from now on in the hope of the resurrection.

*13. Mary of Magdala and then Peter and John come to Jesus' tomb.

20 ¹ It was very early on the first day of the week and still dark, when Mary of Magdala came to the tomb. She saw that the stone had been moved away from the tomb ² and came running to Simon Peter and the other disciple, the one

Jesus loved. 'They have taken the Lord out of the tomb,' she said, 'and we don't know where they have put him.'

³ So Peter set out with the other disciple to go to the tomb. ⁴ They ran together, but the other disciple, running faster than Peter, reached the tomb first; ⁵ he bent down and saw the linen cloths lying on the ground, but did not go in. ⁶ Simon Peter who was following now came up, went right into the tomb, saw the linen cloths on the ground, ⁷ and also the cloth that had been over his head; this was not with the linen cloths but rolled up in a place by itself. ⁸ Then the other disciple who had reached the tomb first also went in; he saw and he believed. ⁹ Till this moment they had failed to understand the teaching of scripture, that he must rise from the dead. ¹⁰ The disciples then went home again.

John stresses Mary's haste, and Peter's and John's. They all run. John is the fastest, probably because he is the youngest; but he does not go into the tomb. Perhaps fear and respect prevent him. Peter, of course, with his usual impetuosity, goes in at once. But we have no reason to think that he believed in his Master's resurrection from that very moment. It is only said of the other disciple, in the singular, that 'He saw and he believed.'

Lord Jesus, you have never stopped asking your disciples to believe in you. Like Peter, we often hesitate in front of the empty tomb and wish that we were able to see you.

Help us to believe, like John, in your living presence, especially in the face of death and when everything seems dark. Help us to believe confidently, trustingly and straightforwardly in you.

*14. The Risen Jesus appears to Mary of Magdala.

20 ¹¹ Meanwhile Mary stayed outside near the tomb, weeping. Then, still weeping, she stooped to look inside, ¹² and saw two angels in white sitting where the body of Jesus had been, one at the head, the other at the feet. ¹³ They said, 'Woman, why are you weeping?' 'They have taken my Lord away,' she replied, 'and I don't know where they have put him.' ¹⁴ As she said this she turned round and

saw Jesus standing there, though she did not recognize him.
¹⁵ Jesus said, 'Woman, why are you weeping? Who are you looking for?' Supposing him to be the gardener, she said, 'Sir, if you have taken him away, tell me where you have put him, and I will go and remove him.' ¹⁶ Jesus said, 'Mary!' She knew him then and said to him in Hebrew, 'Rabbuni!' – which means Master. ¹⁷ Jesus said to her, 'Do not cling to me, because I have not yet ascended to the Father. But go and find the brothers, and tell them: I am ascending to my Father and your Father, to my God and your God.' ¹⁸ So Mary of Magdala went and told the disciples that she had seen the Lord and that he had said these things to her.

So Mary is standing alone by the tomb, weeping. She is not hoping for anything or expecting anything, she does not believe; she only wants to find her Master's body and give it a dignified burial. And Jesus calls her by name. We can imagine her throwing herself at his feet, trying to embrace them again and wash them with her tears. Jesus calms her, but their intimacy will not be fully regained until much later, in the Father's kingdom. Her task now is to be a diligent messenger, an apostle above all the others, the first to announce the shattering news which is going to shake the world: Christ is risen.

Risen Lord Jesus, you did not let Mary of Magdala recognize you at once. You wanted her to look for you, you wanted her to control her feelings . . .

Show us how to persevere and be steadfast and live in faith; teach us to love you more than any display of feeling could show. Help us to recognize you alive in all our fellow men, and keep us in the hope of seeing you face to face in the Father's kingdom.

Conclusion: **The Risen Jesus appears to the disciples.**

20 ¹⁹ In the evening of that same day, the first day of the week, the doors were closed in the room where the disciples were, for fear of the Jews. Jesus came and stood among them. He said to them, 'Peace be with you,' ²⁰ and showed them his hands and his side. The disciples were filled with joy

when they saw the Lord, ²¹ and he said to them again, 'Peace be with you.

> 'As the Father sent me,
> so am I sending you.'

²² After saying this he breathed on them and said:

> 'Receive the Holy Spirit.
> ²³ For those whose sins you forgive,
> they are forgiven;
> for those whose sins you retain,
> they are retained.'

²⁴ Thomas, called the Twin, who was one of the Twelve, was not with them when Jesus came. ²⁵ When the disciples said, 'We have seen the Lord,' he answered: 'Unless I see the holes that the nails made in his hands and can put my finger into the holes they made, and unless I can put my hand into his side, I refuse to believe.' ²⁶ Eight days later the disciples were in the house again and Thomas was with them. The doors were closed, but Jesus came in and stood among them. 'Peace be with you,' he said. ²⁷ Then he spoke to Thomas. 'Put your finger here; look, here are my hands. Give me your hand; put it into my side. Doubt no longer but believe.' ²⁸ Thomas replied, 'My Lord and my God!' ²⁹ Jesus said to him:

> 'You believe because you can see me.
> Happy are those who have not seen and yet believe.'

'My Lord and my God!' This is the only place in the whole Gospel where Jesus is addressed as 'my God'. Thomas has touched Jesus' wounds. He has touched only the human being in him, yet this contact makes him believe in the divinity of his Lord. He has been more incredulous than any of the others, but when faith does come to him, it takes him further than any of them into the mystery of his Master. Jesus' last words are addressed to us, the Christians of the future: 'Happy are those who will believe without seeing me.' Happy indeed are those who believe, as St John said, that Jesus is the Christ, the Son of God, because in believing this they have life through the Risen Lord.

Lord Jesus, you gave the Holy Spirit to your disciples on the day of your resurrection.

Give us this Spirit of power and love, that it may keep us in peace and make us grow in faith. And may our joy be to share with our fellow men in your eternal life.

A Traditional Road to the Cross using

St John

1. Jesus is condemned to death.

19 ⁴ Pilate came outside again and said to them, 'Look, I am going to bring him out to you to let you see that I find no case.' ⁵ Jesus then came out wearing the crown of thorns and the purple robe. Pilate said, 'Here is the man.' ⁶ When they saw him the chief priests and the guards shouted, 'Crucify him! Crucify him!' Pilate said, 'Take him yourselves and crucify him: I can find no case against him.' ⁷ 'We have a Law,' the Jews replied, 'and according to that Law he ought to die, because he has claimed to be the Son of God.'

⁸ When Pilate heard them say this his fears increased. ⁹ Re-entering the Praetorium, he said to Jesus, 'Where do you come from?' But Jesus made no answer. ¹⁰ Pilate then said to him, 'Are you refusing to speak to me? Surely you know I have power to release you and I have power to crucify you?' ¹¹ 'You would have no power over me,' replied Jesus, 'if it had not been given you from above; that is why the one who handed me over to you has the greater guilt.'

¹² From that moment Pilate was anxious to set him free, but the Jews shouted, 'If you set him free you are no friend of Caesar's; anyone who makes himself king is defying Caesar.' ¹³ Hearing these words, Pilate had Jesus brought out, and seated himself on the chair of judgment at a place called the Pavement, in Hebrew Gabbatha. ¹⁴ It was Passover Preparation Day, about the sixth hour. 'Here is your king,' said Pilate to the Jews. ¹⁵ 'Take him away, take him away!' they said. 'Crucify him!' 'Do you want me to crucify your king?' said Pilate. The chief priests answered, 'We

have no king except Caesar.' ¹⁶ So in the end Pilate handed him over to them to be crucified.

'Here is your king', said Pilate. Jesus did not allow himself to be recognized as king except in humility, as on the morning of Palm Sunday when he entered Jerusalem riding on an ass and with children shouting around him. And now it is as a helpless prisoner that he says to Pilate: 'It is as you say it. I am a king', when he is bound and crowned with thorns. And St John records words which assume a weighty importance in this tragic context: 'All who are on the side of truth listen to my voice.' That can only mean that once again the Gospel is inviting the believer to listen humbly and quietly, and to meditate seriously on the most disconcerting fact of all: that the greatest failure is the greatest victory; that the cross has to come before the resurrection, and that ignominious death is the gateway to true life.

O God our Father, we kneel before your Son who was condemned to death and pray for all those who are unjustly condemned.

Help them and grant them your grace. May justice and brotherly love reign at last among all men.

*2. Jesus is made to carry his cross.

19 ¹⁶ They then took charge of Jesus, ¹⁷ and carrying his own cross he went out of the city to the place of the skull or, as it was called in Hebrew, Golgotha.

The sad procession leaves Jerusalem – executions always took place outside the city. But more important than this commonplace event is the fact that in turning his back for ever on the sacred city of Judaism, Jesus shows that the new covenant is being sealed. Carrying his cross on his own shoulders, Jesus goes away from the city which would not receive him. From now on, there will be no one place in the world favoured by the presence of God, no one nation which has a covenant with him. According to his own words, it is the whole of humankind whom Christ, the true Shepherd, will gather together by giving his life for them:

10 ¹⁴ I am the good shepherd;
  I know my own
  and my own know me,
 ¹⁵ just as the Father knows me
  and I know the Father;
  and I lay down my life for my sheep.
 ¹⁶ And there are other sheep I have
  that are not of this fold,
  and these I have to lead as well.
  They too will listen to my voice,
  and there will be only one flock,
  and one shepherd.
 ¹⁷ The Father loves me,
  because I lay down my life
  in order to take it up again.

O God our Father, we kneel before Jesus as he is mocked, ridiculed and burdened with his cross, and we pray for all those who are scorned, misunderstood and persecuted.

May they unite their sufferings with the cross of your Son Jesus, and walk with him where true life may be found.

And we pray for all the nations of the world. May they be gathered at last into one flock, where there shall be one Shepherd.

*3. Jesus falls for the first time.

Jesus said to his disciples:

12 ²³ 'Now the hour has come
    for the Son of Man to be glorified.
  ²⁴ I tell you, most solemnly,
    unless a wheat grain falls on the ground and dies,
    it remains only a single grain;
    but if it dies,
    it yields a rich harvest.
  ²⁵ Anyone who loves his life loses it;
    anyone who hates his life in this world
    will keep it for the eternal life.
  ²⁶ If a man serves me, he must follow me,

> wherever I am, my servant will be there too.
> If anyone serves me, my Father will honour him.
> ²⁷ Now my soul is troubled.
> What shall I say:
> Father, save me from this hour?
> But it was for this very reason that I have come to this hour.
> ²⁸ Father, glorify your name!'

Jesus is on the earth like a grain of wheat. It has to die, unless it is going to remain only a single grain . . . He is not spared the anguish, but however it may seem, God has not abandoned him. Jesus falls, but he knows that he will rise up again and draw all men to him. Perhaps for us, our own cross, and our fall under its weight, may be a time of testing, or illness, or of turning away from Christ; it may also be humble and constant concern to be of service to our unfortunate fellow men. As Christ's cross is his glory, so our own glory is to put ourselves in Christ's hands so that he may teach us to give ourselves day after day.

O God our Father, we kneel before Jesus as he sinks to the ground, and pray for all those who are seriously ill or dying.

Comfort them as they approach death. Keep them in trust and hope by showing them the richness of the gift you have given them – the gift of hope in Christ.

*4. Jesus meets his mother.

> 19 ²⁵ Near the cross of Jesus stood his mother and his mother's sister, Mary the wife of Clopas, and Mary of Magdala. ²⁶ Seeing his mother and the disciple he loved standing near her, Jesus said to his mother, 'Woman, this is your son.' ²⁷ Then to the disciple he said, 'This is your mother.' And from that moment the disciple made a place for her in his home.

Jesus entrusted John to Mary and Mary to John. He did more. He entrusted John to Mary as a son to his mother. It was his wish that there should be a real mother-son relationship between them, over and above the ties of friendship and respect which already linked them. The disciple whom he loved is the representative of all the faithful, so by this action the crucified Jesus has entrusted all his followers to his mother and asked them to think of her as their mother. In this way Mary is in some measure made a partner in her son's work, and the faithful are invited to accept her as a son would, particularly at those times in their lives when they are bowed down under the weight of their cross.

O God our Father, we pray for all mothers and all fathers who watch their children die.

May they live in the hope of seeing them again with you. And may their friends and neighbours see how to embrace them and welcome them as John did the Virgin Mary.

*5. Simon helps Jesus to carry the cross.

St John has not recorded this incident of the passion which the other evangelists relate. He has stressed Jesus' strength and courage rather than his weakness. But Simon remains for us one of the best examples of brotherly love in action, of the kind which Jesus demonstrated to his disciples on the night before his death.

> 13 12 When he had washed their feet and put on his clothes again he went back to the table. 'Do you understand,' he said, 'what I have done to you? 13 You call me Master and Lord, and rightly; so I am. 14 If I, then, the Lord and Master, have washed your feet, you should wash each other's feet. 15 I have given you an example so that you may copy what I have done to you.
>
> 16 'I tell you most solemnly,
> no servant is greater than his master,
> no messenger is greater than the man who sent him.
>
> 17 'Now that you know this, happiness will be yours if you behave accordingly.'

O God our Father, we pray for all those who are being subjected to trial and suffering.

Show us how to help them carry their cross.
Teach us to love them as Christ Jesus loves them.

6. Veronica wipes the face of Jesus.

Veronica's action is not mentioned in the Gospels, but it reminds us of another woman's gesture about which St John tells us.

> 12 [1] Six days before the Passover, Jesus went to Bethany, where Lazarus was, whom he had raised from the dead. [2] They gave a dinner for him there; Martha waited on them and Lazarus was among those at table. [3] Mary brought in a pound of very costly ointment, pure nard, and with it anointed the feet of Jesus, wiping them with her hair; the house was full of the scent of the ointment. [4] Then Judas Iscariot – one of his disciples, the man who was to betray him – said, [5] 'Why wasn't this ointment sold for three hundred denarii, and the money given to the poor?' [6] He said this, not because he cared about the poor, but because he was a thief; he was in charge of the common fund and used to help himself to the contributions. [7] So Jesus said, 'Leave her alone; she had to keep this scent for the day of my burial. [8] You have the poor with you always, you will not always have me.'
>
> [9] Meanwhile a large number of Jews heard that he was there and came not only on account of Jesus but also to see Lazarus whom he had raised from the dead. [10] Then the chief priests decided to kill Lazarus as well, [11] since it was on his account that many of the Jews were leaving them and believing in Jesus.

From an ordinary person's point of view, Judas is quite right; Mary's action was wasteful. But he has not understood that someone who loves deeply does not count the cost. No more did Jesus count the cost when he gave his life. He gave everything because he loved without reserve. Do we know how to follow his example?

O God our Father, we pray for all those who are sick, for those who look after them, for doctors, and for all those who watch beside their suffering brothers.

> *May all they do be in a spirit of friendship and support, of respect and brotherly love – that care of which so many men and women are deprived.*
>
> *And may each one of us be able to open our hearts generously and without counting the cost, and give ourselves as Jesus Christ gave himself.*

*7. Jesus falls for the second time.

Let us kneel before Jesus, crushed by the wood of the cross, and remember what he had said to his disciples.

> 14 27 Peace I bequeath to you,
> my own peace I give you,
> a peace the world cannot give, this is my gift to you.
> Do not let your hearts be troubled or afraid.
> 28 You heard me say:
> I am going away, and shall return.
> If you loved me you would have been glad to know
> that I am going to the Father,
> for the Father is greater than I.
> 29 I have told you this now before it happens,
> so that when it does happen you may believe.
> 30 I shall not talk with you any longer,
> because the prince of this world is on his way.
> He has no power over me,
> 31 but the world must be brought to know that I love the Father
> and that I am doing exactly what the Father told me.
> Come now, let us go.

'I have told you this now so that when it does happen you may believe.' Amongst the small group of friends who follow him into the midst of the insults and gibes of the crowd, who still believes in Jesus? His mother? The beloved disciple? One or other of the women who have shown him so much love? Do they cherish in the depths of their hearts this peace which he promised them? But isn't it at the worst moments when we have most need of God? Isn't it when the desolation is deepest that we need to ask for his peace?

O God our Father, we pray for all those who work for peace.

In the face of hatred, of divisions, of armed conflicts, of wars and of injustice towards men, let us remember Jesus dying to bring us peace.

Teach us to work passionately and with faith for reconciliation, justice and peace among all people.

*8. Jesus comforts the women of Jerusalem.

It is Luke who tells us of these faithful women. But John tells us of Jesus' conversation with a woman of Samaria. We can meditate on his words now.

4 ¹⁰ 'If you only knew what God is offering
and who it is that is saying to you:
Give me a drink,
you would have been the one to ask,
and he would have given you living water.'
. . . .
¹³ 'Whoever drinks this water
will get thirsty again;
¹⁴ but anyone who drinks the water that I shall give
will never be thirsty again:
the water that I shall give
will turn into a spring inside him, welling up to eternal life.'
. . . .
²¹ 'Believe me, woman, the hour is coming
when you will worship the Father
neither on this mountain nor in Jerusalem.
²² You worship what you do not know;
we worship what we do know:
for salvation comes from the Jews.
²³ But the hour will come – in fact it is here already –
when true worshippers will worship the Father in spirit and truth:
that is the kind of worshipper
the Father wants.
²⁴ God is spirit,
and those who worship
must worship in spirit and truth.'

The hour is coming. The hour of Jesus; the hour of his passion, and that also means his glory. To worship God in spirit and in truth, we have to live through the hour of his passion. To be washed by the living water promised by Jesus we have to receive the water which flowed from his side, pierced by the centurion's spear. And yet there is nothing to fear, since it is Jesus himself who gives us strength, it is he who comforts us, he who washes us, who shows us love. 'It is not you who have chosen me,' he said, 'but I who have chosen you.'

O God our Father, we pray for all Christian women; our mothers, our wives, our daughters, our sisters.
May the love of the crucified Christ uphold them in their lives. May men honour and respect them and accord them their rightful place in the Church and in the world.

*9. Jesus falls for the third time.

15 ⁹ As the Father has loved me,
   so I have loved you.
   Remain in my love.
¹⁰ If you keep my commandments
   you will remain in my love,
   just as I have kept my Father's commandments
   and remain in his love.
   . . . .
¹² This is my commandment:
   love one another,
   as I have loved you.
¹³ A man can have no greater love
   than to lay down his life for his friends.
¹⁴ You are my friends,
   if you do what I command you.
¹⁵ I shall not call you servants any more,
   because a servant does not know
   his master's business;
   I call you friends,
   because I have made known to you
   everything I have learnt from my Father.

> ¹⁶ You did not choose me,
> no, I chose you;
> and I commissioned you
> to go out and to bear fruit,
> fruit that will last;
> and then the Father will give you
> anything you ask him in my name.
> ¹⁷ What I command you
> is to love one another.

As we kneel before Jesus overwhelmed by the cross, we may meditate on this passage that John has passed on to us, which is none other than a hymn to the love of God, to the love of Christ and to the love of our fellow men. Christ's last commandment was to love in such a way that the warring factions of obedience and freedom give way to open heartedness, peace and inner joy. And, at the same time, like a ceaseless refrain, there is the comparison with Jesus: 'Love, as I have loved you.' And that recalls both the commonplace gift, the gift of washing the feet, and also the supreme gift, that of life, that of great love. Can we love every day in all the little things as well as in the big and important ones?

Let us pray that we may learn to love.

O God our Father, we pray for those whom we love and for those from whom we are divided.

May we follow Jesus' example and open our hearts and our hands to those who are most poor, most wretched, most despised.

May Christ's love one day transform the world!

10. Jesus is stripped of his clothing.

> 19 ²³ When the soldiers had finished crucifying Jesus they took his clothing and divided it into four shares, one for each soldier. His undergarment was seamless, woven in one piece from neck to hem; ²⁴ so they said to one another, 'Instead of tearing it, let's throw dice to decide who is to have it.' In this way the words of scripture were fulfilled:
>
> They shared out my clothing among them.
> They cast lots for my clothes.

This is exactly what the soldiers did.

The soldiers cast lots for Jesus' clothes, thus fulfilling a prophecy of Psalm 22. This is the psalm which begins with the words: 'My God, my God, why have you forsaken me?', which Matthew and Mark have recorded as being among the last words spoken by the crucified Jesus. John does not quote this cry of desolation. He only uses that part of the psalm which demonstrates that Jesus is the awaited Messiah.

The seamless garment woven in one piece was one which the high priest wore when he offered the sacrifice. To the layman, the fact that Jesus wore one on the day of his death could seem a sheer coincidence; but it was certainly not for John who, at the time he writes, regards Jesus as the one true priest and his death as the one true sacrifice which can bring together all the scattered children of God.

O God our Father, we kneel before Jesus, stripped and made bare, and pray for the most wretched of mankind; the children of the African deserts, the outcasts of India, the starving natives of Brazil, the orphans and widows of El Salvador – all those in the world who have neither clothing, nor houses, nor food, nor work.

Teach us to share what we have with them. Show us how to help them. May all the people of the developed countries be led to identify themselves with those who are the most poor.

*11. Jesus is nailed to the cross.

19 ¹⁷ They then took charge of Jesus, and carrying his own cross he went out of the city to the place of the skull or, as it was called in Hebrew, Golgotha, ¹⁸ where they crucified him with two others, one on either side with Jesus in the middle. ¹⁹ Pilate wrote out a notice and had it fixed to the cross; it ran: 'Jesus the Nazarene, King of the Jews'. ²⁰ This notice was read by many of the Jews, because the place where Jesus was crucified was not far from the city, and the writing was in Hebrew, Latin and Greek. ²¹ So the Jewish chief priests said to Pilate, 'You should not write "King of the Jews", but "This man said: I am King of the

Jews".' ²² Pilate answered, 'What I have written, I have written.'

We kneel in front of Jesus' cross at the time of faith and prayer. As he had said to his disciples:

> 16 ³² Listen; the time will come – in fact it has come already –
> when you will be scattered, each going his own way
> and leaving me alone.
> And yet I am not alone.
> because the Father is with me.
> ³³ I have told you all this
> so that you may find peace in me.
> In the world you will have trouble,
> but be brave:
> I have conquered the world.

As we kneel before the crucified Lord our sadness cannot be without hope. We believe in the resurrection, in Christ's and in the resurrection of all men whom he has served through his cross. Christ is the victor over all the powers of evil, and we continue the battle with him.

O God our Father, we kneel before our crucified king and pray for all sinners, as we know ourselves to be.

Grant us your pardon and your mercy.

Make the love of Jesus known to those who have never felt it. Bring home to you the prodigal son, the lost sheep, the thief and the man condemned to death.

May all people regain the hope of one day being victors with Christ in your kingdom.

*12. Jesus dies on the cross.

19 ²⁸ After this, Jesus knew that everything had now been completed, and to fulfil the scripture perfectly he said:

'I am thirsty.'

²⁹ A jar full of vinegar stood there, so putting a sponge soaked in the vinegar on a hyssop stick they held it up to his mouth.³⁰ After Jesus had taken the vinegar he said, 'It is accomplished'; and bowing his head he gave up his spirit.

³¹ It was Preparation Day, and to prevent the bodies remaining on the cross during the sabbath – since that sabbath was a day of special solemnity – the Jews asked Pilate to have the legs broken and the bodies taken away. ³² Consequently the soldiers came and broke the legs of the first man who had been crucified with him and then of the other. ³³ When they came to Jesus, they found he was already dead, and so instead of breaking his legs ³⁴ one of the soldiers pierced his side with a lance; and immediately there came out blood and water.

'It is accomplished,' said Jesus. That is to say, 'I have completed the task my Father gave me.' So he is able to breathe his last. This breath of life which comes down from the cross is the Holy Spirit which he sends into the world, the Spirit which is the source of life, the Spirit which will rekindle the disciples' passion and build up the new People of God, the Church of Jesus Christ. This Church rests on the two great sacraments of baptism and the eucharist as on two foundation stones. They are symbolized by the water and the blood which flow from the pierced heart of the crucified Jesus. The blood is the visible sign of the reality and the boundless generosity of his sacrifice. The water is that living water gushing forth which is life eternal, and which John has already said is the Holy Spirit poured out abundantly upon all believers.

O God our Father, we pray for all mankind today, yesterday and tomorrow, of all races and of all nations. For their sake, Jesus allowed himself to be handed over to his executioners and to suffer the agony of the cross.

Through your passion and through your blood shed for us, may your Holy Spirit encompass the world and make it new with mercy, love and peace.

13. Jesus is lifted down from the cross.

19 ³⁵ This is the evidence of one who saw it – trustworthy evidence, and he knows he speaks the truth – and he gives it so that you may believe as well. ³⁶ Because all this happened to fulfil the words of scripture:

Not one bone of his will be broken;

³⁷ and again, in another place scripture says:

They will look on the one whom they have pierced.

³⁸ After this, Joseph of Arimathaea, who was a disciple of Jesus – though a secret one because he was afraid of the Jews – asked Pilate to let him remove the body of Jesus. Pilate gave permission, so they came and took it away. ³⁹ Nicodemus came as well – the same one who had first come to Jesus at night-time – and he brought a mixture of myrrh and aloes, weighing about a hundred pounds. ⁴⁰ They took the body of Jesus and wrapped it with the spices in linen cloths, following the Jewish burial custom. ⁴¹ At the place where he had been crucified there was a garden, and in this garden a new tomb in which no one had yet been buried. ⁴² Since it was the Jewish Day of Preparation and the tomb was near at hand, they laid Jesus there.

John ends his narrative of the passion on a very peaceful note. He gives a straightforward account of what happens, and the only observation he makes is about faith. He says: 'He who saw these things gives evidence so that you may believe as well.' But what does it mean to believe? For him, faith is not primarily clinging to a collection of revealed truths, but rather confident trust in another, in God. When we kneel in front of Christ's cross and John asks us to believe, it is above all an invitation to put our lives into God's hands, as Christ himself delivered his to his Father. He does not give us a lot of reasons; he simply asks us to look upon the crucified Christ. Indeed, our gaze ought like his to be full of faith, love and hope. Such a gaze can make it possible for us in our turn to pass through tribulation or grief, knowing that they are the road which leads to the resurrection and to true life. 'I am the Resurrection and the Life,' says Jesus to Martha before raising her brother Lazarus. St John echoes this when writing at the end of his Gospel: 'All this is recorded so that you may believe that Jesus is the Christ, the Son of God, and that believing this you may have life through his name.'

O God our Father, as we look on Jesus subjected to death, we pray in faith for all our family and friends who have died.

Remember, too, all those who have died in so many wars and all those who are forgotten and for whom no one prays. Gather them all to you in rest and peace and true life with Jesus Christ our Lord.

*14. Jesus rests in the expectation of the resurrection.

As we kneel in front of Jesus' tomb, it is not a time of desolation but of hope. Because the tomb will open, and Christ will burst forth alive. What does he ask of us in the meantime? First of all to believe in him. Let us recall his conversation with Martha after the death of Lazarus.

> 11 21 Martha said to Jesus, 'If you had been here, my brother would not have died, 22 but I know that, even now, whatever you ask of God, he will grant you.' 23 'Your brother,' said Jesus to her, 'will rise again.' 24 Martha said, 'I know he will rise again at the resurrection on the last day.' 25 Jesus said:
>
> 'I am the resurrection.
> If anyone believes in me, even though he dies he will live,
> 26 and whoever lives and believes in me
> will never die.
> Do you believe this?'
>
> 27 'Yes, Lord,' she said, 'I believe that you are the Christ, the Son of God, the one who was to come into this world.'

The words which Martha was able to say before her brother's tomb, Thomas the unbelieving disciple will declare still more forcefully, and his 'yes' will lead us to join him in saying without fear or hesitation: 'My Lord and my God!'

O God our Father, we give you thanks for the passion and death of Jesus, because we know that there is no greater love than to give our life for those we love. And we bless you because we believe that he has risen to give us life with you and to lead us, through the Holy Spirit, to the fullness of your love.

Index

Index of Stations and Passages

The Road to the Cross according to St Matthew

Introduction: The transfiguration: Jesus sees in advance the glory of the resurrection. 17.1–9 — 7
1. The Jewish leaders and Judas surrender Jesus for the price of a slave. 26.1–16 — 8
2. Jesus celebrates his last supper where he offers himself for the forgiveness of sins, while Judas betrays him. 26.17–29 — 9
3. On the way to Gethsemane, Jesus tells Peter that he will disown him. 26.30–35 — 11
4. In Gethsemane, Jesus is afraid of death and seeks help from his disciples. But he accepts the will of the Father. 26.36–46 — 12
5. Jesus, when arrested, refuses to use his divine power. 26.47–56 — 13
6. In front of the high priest, Jesus says who he is. 26.57–68 — 14
7. Peter disowns his master. 26.69–75 — 15
*8. Judas despairs of Christ's forgiveness. 27.1–10 — 16
9. In spite of his wife's intervention, Pilate condemns Jesus Christ and frees Jesus Barabbas. 27.11–26 — 17
10. Jesus is crowned with thorns and given a mock sceptre. 27.27–31 — 18
11. The Righteous Man suffers and is crucified. 27.32–44 — 19
*12. Jesus' death on the cross signals the new age. 27.45–54 — 20
13. The chief priests put a guard on Jesus' tomb. 27.55–66 — 21
*14. The open tomb brings in the new age. 28.1–10 — 22
Conclusion: The glorified Jesus send his disciples into all the world. 28.16–20 — 23

The Road to the Cross according to St Mark

Introduction: Through the transfiguration, God gives Jesus the assurance of his love. 9.2–9 — 27
1. The chief priests have decided to put Jesus to death. A woman anticipates his burial by pouring ointment over his head. 14.1–9 — 28

2. While Judas is betraying him, Jesus makes preparations for his last supper. 14.10–16 — 29
3. Jesus gives himself to the disciples in his last supper; one of them betrays him and another will deny him. 14.17–25 — 30
4. Jesus declares that Peter will disown him. 14.26–31 — 31
5. Jesus suffers agony in Gethsemane. 14.32–42 — 32
6. Abandoned by everyone and arrested, alone Jesus undergoes his passion. 14.43–52 — 33
7. In front of the high priest, Jesus proclaims who he is. 14.53–65 — 34
8. Peter disowns his master. 14.66–72 — 36
9. Jesus, the king of the Jews, is rejected by the Jews and condemned by Pilate. 15.1–15 — 36
10. The Roman soldiers mock the king of the Jews. 15.16–20 — 38
11. Simon of Cyrene is made to carry Jesus' cross. 15.20–22 — 39
12. The Messiah, the king of the Jews, is crucified. 15.23–32 — 39
13. In dying on the cross, Jesus opens the Temple to all people. 15.33–41 — 40
14. Jesus is laid in the tomb. 15.42–47 — 42
Conclusion: Go and tell the world that he who was crucified is risen! 16.1–8 — 42

The Road to the Cross according to St Luke

Introduction: In the transfiguration, the disciples see Jesus' glory. 9.28–36 — 47
1. Jesus longs to eat the passover with his disciples. 22.1–7, 14–20 — 48
*2. After supper, Jesus gives his last commands to his disciples. 22.21–34 — 49
3. On the Mount of Olives, Jesus, the new Elijah, fights his supreme battle. 22.39–46 — 50
4. Jesus is arrested. 22.47–53 — 51
5. Peter, who denied Jesus, is transformed by a look from him. 22.54–65 — 52
6. Before the Sanhedrin, Jesus declares himself to be the Messiah and the Son of God. 22.66–71 — 53
*7. Pilate recognizes Jesus to be innocent and sends him to Herod. 23.1–12 — 54
8. Pilate delivers Jesus up to the whim of his enemies. 23.13–25 — 55
*9. Simon from Cyrene and the women take part in Jesus' passion. 23.26–32 — 56

INDEX OF STATIONS AND PASSAGES

*10. Jesus is crucified. His first words are of forgiveness. 23.33–38	57
*11. The next words of the crucified Jesus open the gates of Paradise to a criminal. 23.39–43	58
*12. Jesus speaks to his Father from the cross. 23.44–49	59
13. The peace of the tomb. 23.50–56	60
*14. The tomb is open! The Lord Jesus is alive! 24.1–12	61
*Conclusion: Two disciples meet with Jesus on the road to Emmaus. 24.13–35	62

The Road to the Cross according to St John

*Introduction: On his entry into Jerusalem on Palm Sunday, Jesus announces his death and his glory. 12.20–33	67
*1. Jesus washes his disciples' feet. 13.1–17	68
*2. Before enduring his passion, Jesus prays for his disciples. 17.1–6, 18–23	70
3. Jesus allows himself to be arrested. 18.1–12	71
4. Jesus appears before the Jewish high priest. 18.13–14, 19–24	72
5. Jesus is led before Pilate. 18.28–40	73
6. The soldiers hail Jesus as 'king'. 19.1–5	75
*7. Jesus is proclaimed 'king' by Pilate. 19.6–16	75
8. The crucified king. 19.16–24	77
*9. Jesus and his mother. 19.25–27	78
*10. Jesus dies on the cross. 19.28–30	79
*11. A soldier pierces Jesus' side with a lance. 19.31–37	79
12. Jesus is laid in the tomb. 19.38–42	81
*13. Mary of Magdala and then Peter and John come to Jesus' tomb. 20.1–10	81
*14. The Risen Jesus appears to Mary of Magdala. 20.11–18	82
*Conclusion: The Risen Jesus appears to the disciples. 20.19–29	83

A Traditional Road to the Cross using St John

1. Jesus is condemned to death. 19.4–16	89
*2. Jesus is made to carry his cross. 19.16–17; 10.14–17	90
*3. Jesus falls for the first time. 12.23–28	91
*4. Jesus meets his mother. 19.25–27	92
*5. Simon helps Jesus to carry the cross. 13.12–17	93
6. Veronica wipes the face of Jesus. 12.1–11	94
*7. Jesus falls for the second time. 14.27–31	95
*8. Jesus comforts the women of Jerusalem. 4.10, 13–14, 21–24	96

*9. Jesus falls for the third time. 15.9–17	97
10. Jesus is stripped of his clothing. 19.23–24	98
*11. Jesus is nailed to the cross. 19.17–22; 16.32–33	99
*12. Jesus dies on the cross. 19.28–34	100
13. Jesus is lifted down from the cross. 19.35–42	102
*14. Jesus rests in the expectation of the resurrection. 11.21–27	103

www.ingramcontent.com/pod-product-compliance
Lightning Source LLC
Chambersburg PA
CBHW071407290426
44108CB00014B/1720